Who
You Really Are

Who You Really Are

And How Reality Actually Works

ANDREW SOLTAU

AVANT GARDE SCIENCE

AVANT GARDE SCIENCE

Bath

www.avantgardescience.com

ISBN 978-0-9539518-4-0

Contents

Appendices

"We live in the wake of a physics revolution comparable to the Copernican demolition of the anthropocentric world - a revolution which began with the theory of relativity and quantum mechanics in the first decade of this century and which has left most educated people behind."

Heinz Pagels (1982)

Preface

The completion of the physics revolution Pagels describes, quoted above, engages a profound transformation in human nature. This new worldview naturally resolves many of the intractable problems facing our human race. The beauty is that anyone who participates benefits tremendously. Scientific enlightenment spells power and freedom.

What is reality? Who am I really? We are more likely to wonder what is the meaning of life? What happens after I die? Throughout the ages attempts to answer such questions have spawned philosophies and religions, and at their best these provided both individual solace and a basis for social order. But now that we have developed the marvel of modern rational science, this new body of knowledge has provided austere straightforward answers. Reality is the physical world, plain and simple, and we are just really clever naked apes. Death is the end. The meaning is what you make of it. Spiritual principles seem to be discredited, leaving the world a less enchanted place. But the full meaning of the new physics is only just beginning to dawn. It is truly transformative. It is also very weird.

What is not in doubt is that our old ideas do not fit. The ordinary world we are familiar with is the world of classical 'Newtonian mechanics'. This defines formal rules for how the ordinary world works, how fast an apple falls and how to make steam engines. These are the rules of the everyday reality on which our intuitive sense of how the world works is based. But the new physics of Einstein's relativity and quantum theory shows us that these rules are not fundamental. Beyond the bounds of scale of everyday experience, utterly different types of phenomena rule. And the world these new rules define is so weird that even the greatest scientists have not been able to comprehend it. As physicist Nick Herbert wrote in *Quantum Reality*:

> Wrenched out of centuries-old thought patterns, physicists of a century ago found themselves compelled to embrace a new metaphysics. The distress which this reorientation caused continues to the present day. Basically physicists have suffered a severe loss: their hold on reality. (1985, 15)

In other words, the new physics tells us things so strange that nobody has been able to grasp it despite a century of expert investigation.

In fact, however, the physicists have not only discovered the nature of the reality defined by the new physics but described it in detail, but there has been no framework in which to understand what it really means. This is the 'holographic universe'. The problem is it makes no sense. As physicist Robbert Dijkgraaf describes:

> What's happening in space is, in some sense, all described in terms of a screen outside here. The ultimate description of reality resides on this screen. (2019)

This is the holographic principle of physicist Gerard t'Hooft, discovered in 1993. As physicist Lee Smolin writes, this is for sure:

> ... an idea which at first seems too crazy to be true, but which survives all our attempts to disprove it. (2000, 178)

The resolution is simple, but a major leap. This is not a fiendishly counter-intuitive redefinition of the ordinary world, yet to be comprehended, but a completely different type of world. This is what makes sense of the physics and explains the major paradoxes. Physical reality itself is the ordinary world, as we naturally assume. Modern physics describes the nature of this world precisely. But the resulting physical reality in which one actually lives is a holographic universe.

The idea that reality is very different to the standard concept of the world has been put forward again and again over the years. The first major interpretation of quantum theory, the 'Copenhagen interpretation' of the 1920s, held that the world is only 'determinate', meaning physically real, where it is observed. The latest interpretation, 'Quantum Bayesianism', demonstrates this principle with a mind-bending twist. The world is only determinate where it is personally observed by you. And as the authors state, this means we live in personal, parallel realities. Bizarre though it sounds, this has now been demonstrated in a recent leading-edge physics experiment. This confirms the principle of 'Wigner's Friend' discovered in 1961, which means exactly this. We live in different versions of physical reality. This is the direct implication of taking the experimental evidence at face value.

What seems to have passed unnoticed is that this means each physical reality is only determinate on the observed surface. In other words, this is the holographic universe. The 'screen outside' is the outer limit of each individual's perception, which is what defines this reality.

So this was discovered some time ago but it made no sense. Analysing it all, I stumbled on the answer. The missing explanatory principle is 'logical type' as described in Part 2. It means that the holographic universe you live in is lots of ordinary worlds all at once, a 'quantum superposition'; and by definition this is only determinate where you have observed it. Of course it seems crazy but this is what we should be expecting. As physicist Steven Hawking said in *The Grand Design*, many notions in today's science seem to violate common sense:

> But common sense is based on everyday experience, not upon the universe as it is revealed by the marvels of technologies such as those that allow us to gaze deep into the atom or back to the early universe. (2010, 15)

What nobody seems to have anticipated is that the implications are of tremendous significance in our daily lives. The new worldview is greatly empowering. The nature of the holographic universe means that one is closely connected with one's world, and this reveals why creative visualisation works unreasonably well. Certain great myths describe genuine attributes of how this kind of reality actually operates. Spirit is who we really are, and the great spiritual principles are fundamental to our humanity. This is what separates us from being just biological machines, both with regard to morality and immortality. These intuitions that our ancestors enshrined in spiritual practice are genuine principles in operation in the real world.

The principles that emerge are vital knowledge for humanity because these have the power to resolve our self-induced global catastrophic risks. As environmental advocate Gus Speth famously said:

> I used to think that top environmental problems were biodiversity loss, ecosystem collapse and climate change. I thought that thirty years of good science could address these problems. I was wrong. The top environmental problems are selfishness, greed and apathy, and to deal with these we need a cultural and spiritual transformation. And we scientists don't know how to do that. (2013)

In the light of the concepts presented here we actually do. This is exactly the effect of the new understanding of reality. In the personal world defined by the new physics, and now confirmed in experiment, your world is yourself in another form. It means enlightened self-interest is a fundamental requirement for true success. Logically, the new worldview must surely seed a beneficial cultural revolution.

Why me? Why would the solution be discovered by a retired systems analyst rather than the experts in physics? This is explained by the concept of 'scientific revolution', described in Appendix I. Essentially it means it takes an outsider to see it. I humbly apologise if my tone is dogmatic but from an operational point of view I see the logic as just so obvious. I am some way from neurotypical and I hope you will forgive my awkwardness. Given the very real threats it seems to me we can no longer dilly-dally about the meaning of the superb science while our denial of the logical implications prevents us from saving our global ecology from ruin, and our human race from self-annihilation through a dozen causes. The new worldview shows us we are empowered and we are responsible. The game of life is much greater in scope and vastly more involved than we have conceived. Now it is time to play with a full deck.

PART 1

THE REALITY

"Behind it all is surely an idea so simple, so beautiful, that when we grasp it - in a decade, a century, or a millennium - we will all say to each other, how could it have been otherwise? How could we have been so stupid for so long?"

John Wheeler (1986)

1

Scientific Revolution

Five hundred years ago the astronomer Nicolaus Copernicus set in motion the first great scientific revolution. He established that the Sun is the centre of the solar system, and thus the Earth was never the centre of the universe. Scientific infancy was over.

Three hundred years ago the physics of Newton's laws of motion transformed our scientific understanding of the world. This is now called 'classical physics'. This means that the world is nothing but a huge physical mechanism, like a giant clockwork. This new perspective became the scientific 'paradigm' of the following centuries, the established worldview. There are no ghosts in the machine, nature spirits in the woods or Gods on Mount Olympus. The industrial revolution was born, and a modern culture based around ever-increasingly powerful technology gradually arose.

One hundred years ago the two pillars of the new physics were discovered, quantum theory and relativity. The advance of new technologies was greatly accelerated, culminating in the current information age of global connectivity. But great mysteries remain, not only in quantum theory but in relativity also. This latest revolution is unfinished. Here a working completion is presented.

Chapters 2-8 describe the startling new view of reality that emerges when we take the implications of quantum theory at face value, then we go on to relativity. 'Quantum Bayesianism', the work of a group of physicists headed by Christopher Fuchs, lights the way. First a one-page summary of quantum theory.

Quantum Theory

Quantum theory tells us exactly what physical reality is fundamentally made of, quanta, but exactly what this means is still not clear. For sure, it means the world is not a predictable clockwork domain, but no satisfactory explanation of exactly what it *does* mean has been found. As stated by philosopher of physics Wayne Myrvold:

> Despite its status as a core part of contemporary physics, there is no consensus among physicists or philosophers of physics on the question of what, if anything, the empirical success of quantum theory is telling us about the physical world. (2016)

So what is the big problem with quantum theory? It works perfectly, but it makes no sense. The nature of the quantum is what gives rise to all the problems. What is it exactly? The whole thing is summed up as 'wave-particle duality'. A quantum is defined by a 'wave function', which is a wave of probability. Except when it is observed, and then it becomes a tiny real thing. The wave collapses to produce a submicroscopic particle, such as an electron. Everything not observed stays as a wave of probability, unreal. That is the standard textbook explanation in a nutshell. This is essentially the Copenhagen interpretation that emerged from the 1920s on.

So what *does* it all mean? Is the world really real? Perhaps there is something underlying the wave. It is clear there is not. The only alternative is 'superstrings', and the basic unit exists only in one dimension, so you can hardly call that real. It is all a great mystery.

The working hypothesis is the 'quasi-classical' world of the current scientific worldview, a mashup. Classical because at everyday levels of scale it works according to Newtonian mechanics. The zillions of quanta in any ordinary object average out to classical physics. So the ordinary world we encounter is Newtonian. Quasi, as if, because at very small scales of reality everything is defined solely by quantum probability waves. This is confirmed by a hundred years of experiments. Down at the submicroscopic level of the quantum it is clear that the real world is 'indeterminate', meaning physically uncertain.

QBism

The problem is that this still does not fit all the facts of experiment. This is where Quantum Bayesianism, now called QBism, comes in. This fits the facts perfectly. The brilliant thing is that this resolves all the major issues in quantum theory. As the authors state, QBism:

> ... removes the paradoxes, conundra, and pseudo-problems that have plagued quantum foundations for the past nine decades. (Fuchs et al., 2013, 1)

So it sounds as if it must surely be correct. How did they do it? This is where it gets really weird. QBism simply takes the original Copenhagen interpretation at face value, with a twist. It is all indeterminate, except where *you* observe it. And then it is a solid thing, where you have observed it, and all the rest stays as a wave of probability.

The implication is staggering. Everything you have not observed, no matter how solid and ordinary, is defined solely in terms of probabilities. Whether that charming cafe on the beach is still there, or even what is actually there under your floor are not determinate physical certainties one way or another, but probabilities. That is what QBism means. The real world is made of probabilities, and it somehow turns into determinate physical reality when, and only when, you personally observe it. A bit of explanation about QBism, and 'Bayesian probability', is given in Appendix III.

As you can imagine, there is no end of resistance to this idea. Objectivity seems to be out the window. And technically, it seems to be directly contradicted by the fundamentals of the quasi-classical world. So the concept has been generally ignored. The resolution is that both concepts are correct. The quasi-classical world and the QBism world are both real. It means there are two very different types of real world. As will be shown, the personal world that QBism defines is the holographic universe. This is the nature of the world you live in, taking the implications of quantum theory at face value.

2

The Superworld

The new concept presented here is that there are two completely different types of physical reality. This is the natural meaning of quantum theory as described in detail in Part 2.

Many Worlds

The ordinary physical world that we naturally take for granted is of course the basic reality, but that is only part of the picture. Firstly, modern science shows us that we live in the universe of all possible physical worlds, often referred to as the 'multiverse'. As cosmologist Max Tegmark describes in his article *Parallel Universes* this is:

> ... a direct implication of cosmological observations (2003)

This is the first imagination-wrenching adjustment to our world-view. It means not only is the universe incomprehensibly vast, but also that every possible version of the world exists within it.

So this means that every possible variation of the way things could get played out in reality does actually exist, in a real version of the world, in this universe. This is the famous 'many-worlds' theory.

The next point, which is no less tricky to grasp, is that all these worlds are here and now. Weird though it is, this is the universe as defined by quantum theory as Tegmark also explains. So these worlds are not somewhere else, off in the distance in the cosmos. They are parallel realities, slightly different versions of the whole world, that exist exactly where we are, here and now, like the parallel worlds in Terry Pratchett's *Long Earth* saga.

The final point is every bit as strange. As Tegmark describes, there is a vast number of identical copies of you in the many worlds. This too is just standard physics. Since every possible version of the world exists, every possible version of the world that contains you, just as you are here and now, exists: "A universe must exist for every physical possibility." (Chown, 2001 , 1).

The Indeterminate World

Now for the new explanation. Because all the copies are in the same place at the same time, all the 'copies' are just you. So there *is* only one of you. But this means you are actually living in all these worlds, all at the same time. This is where all the weirdness comes from. This means your physical reality is the superposed sum of all these worlds. Call it a 'superworld'. This domain operates exactly as described by QBism – it is only real where *you* have observed it.

Suppose there is a butterfly perched behind me sunning himself. I cannot see the position of his wings. For every possible position he may have adopted, that is the case in one of the worlds I am in. The net result, in my superworld, is the sum of all these versions of reality, as shown in the last image in Figure 2. So in my superworld, the position of his wings is not just unknown but physically indeterminate. This is the nature of the physical reality I actually encounter.

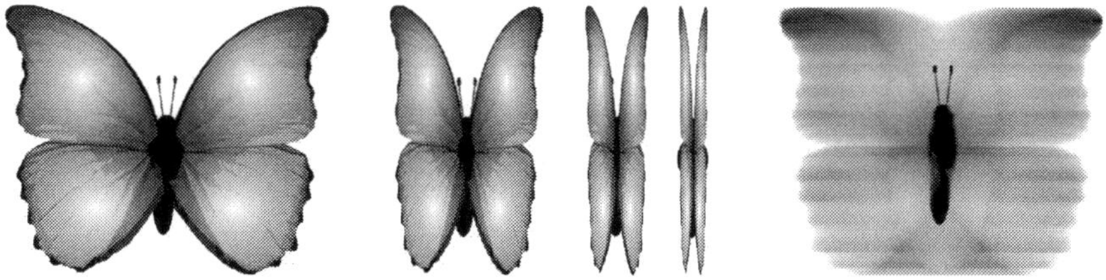

Figure 2 Four possible wing positions, and all possible positions superposed.

It is like a picture produced by a whole lot of slides of that butterfly, each one with the wings in a different position, all stacked up on an overhead projector. All the slightly different images are superimposed. In just the same kind of way, all the worlds in which I exist are superimposed. The result is a different kind of world, a superworld. This is the kind of physical reality in which one actually lives.

Of course, real physical worlds do not sound like the kinds of things that can be superimposed on each other in that sort of way, but exactly this principle is fundamental to modern physics. As described in detail in Part 2, the 'superposition principle' means that any two or more physical systems add together in just the same kind of way as the slides. So superimposed worlds just add together.

The net result is a completely different type of thing to the ordinary world as we naturally imagine it to be. It seems obvious that the real world is an ordinary world, all there, real and solid. And of course it is. But the physical reality you encounter, your superworld, is the simultaneous existence of a great number of worlds, all superposed. As we shall see, the net effect is a holographic universe as described in the Preface. This is the physical form of the QBism world.

The QBism World

The superposition of worlds produces exactly the strange world that QBism describes, but here we have a simple physical basis for this outlandish concept, the 'ontology'. Everything observed is the same in all these worlds, like the body of the butterfly. So when all these worlds are added together these things are 100% real, determinate. But everything not observed is the superposed sum of all the ways it could possibly be, like the wings. In all likelihood the butterfly behind me has his wings wide open for warmth and display, but in my superworld the situation is not just unknown but indeterminate, physically uncertain. Very weird, but this type of world resolves the great paradoxes, as the authors describe, and nothing else does according to a hundred years of research. In other words, this type of world is the only description of physical reality that actually works.

The concept of this indeterminate world has been presented many times over the years. Physicist Lev Vaidman describes this as a 'relative world', meaning the world defined relative to the individual:

> In this world, all objects which the sentient being perceives have definite states, but objects that are not under her observation might be in a superposition of different (classical) states. (2002)

But although this solves the great paradoxes it is studiously ignored because it directly contradicts the current scientific worldview. The ordinary quasi-classical world is the established paradigm.

It Is All Real

The relative world is the type of world now recently confirmed by experiment. This is how reality actually works. The key to the puzzle is that the physics defines two completely different types of world, the ordinary world and the relative world, the superworld, both equally real. This is where QBism falls down. One of the central reasons QBism is not taken seriously is because it denies the existence of the ordinary world. But the ordinary world is all perfectly real. Just as seems obvious, the fundamental physical reality is the ordinary world, the quasi-classical world of modern physics. But the relative world is every bit as real. This is the reality encountered.

The origins of the superworld and its holographic form are described in increasing detail as we go along. The superworld is also referred to here as the QBism world, the personal world and the holographic universe. The implications are huge. As described in the next chapter, it means we live in personal, physical, parallel realities. And as described in Chapter 4, it means one is deeply connected with the whole of the world in which one lives. All this is simply taking the new physics at face value as explained in detail in Part 2.

3

Multi-Solipsism

The further direct implication of QBism is another major departure from the current worldview. The physical reality of the real world is different for different people. As the authors state:

> This means that reality differs from one agent to another. This is not as strange as it may sound. What is real for an agent rests entirely on what that agent experiences, and different agents have different experiences. (Fuchs et al., 2013, 3)

One would think that this bizarre implication directly contradicts the principles of modern physics, but just the opposite is the case. As shown in the famous 'Wigner's friend' thought experiment, put forward in 1961, standard quantum theory means that physical reality is indeed different for different people, 'observer-dependent'. Crucially, this has now been confirmed in experiment by Proietti et al.:

> This result lends considerable strength to interpretations of quantum theory already set in an observer-dependent framework and demands for revision of those which are not. (2019, abstract)

Personal Parallel Realities

It means we live in personal, physical, parallel realities. Of course, it seems so perfectly obvious we are all in the same physical environment. How could that possibly not be the case, especially when we are in direct contact, shaking hands with someone? The answer is that we are, but only with regard to this immediate environment we are both engaged with, here and now. At the same time, other things in each person's physical reality are different.

Say I see a friend coming to meet me. My superworld includes every possible world in which this situation exists. And these different worlds include all the different possible versions of events in her day so far, got the deal of a lifetime, got fired, had an average day and so on. So for me, her day is not just unknown but indeterminate. We live in different superworlds. This is why two people who are obviously in the same ordinary world, seeing, hearing and even touching each other, nonetheless live in different versions of physical reality.

These implications are truly weird, but as Tegmark states, the strange and alien nature of quantum reality should not surprise us:

> Moreover, we should expect quantum mechanics to feel counterintuitive because evolution endowed us with intuition only for those aspects of physics that had survival value for our distant ancestors, such as the trajectories of flying rocks. (2007, 3)

The classical, Newtonian, flying-rock world is how an ordinary physical world works. This is what shapes our intuitions, and forms the basis of the current worldview. But with the advent of quantum theory it becomes clear that the physical reality in which one lives is a totally different type of domain to the ordinary world we naturally assume. And now we have evidence from experimental physics. Reality is observer-dependent, defined only where one has observed it.

Solipsisms

The resulting world is personal in a very absolute way. Since the rules of the indeterminate QBism world apply to everything in reality, they automatically apply to other people as well. This means that only those aspects of another person that you have observed are determinate in your physical reality. Everything else about them is indeterminate. You see only the outside appearance of other people, and so everything else about them, such as what is going on in their minds, is not just unknown but indeterminate. Of course, when we talk to each other we communicate what is going on in our minds, but essentially each person one meets is wholly indeterminate except for what our senses tell us.

The conceptual revolution is profound. This means that the only person completely real and determinate in your physical reality is yourself. This is very like the philosophical concept of solipsism. That holds that I am the only person in reality, the only real entity, and that everything in reality is part of my mind, including you. That is clearly absurd, which is why no one takes it seriously. But the reality in which one lives is actually very like this. I am the only person fully determinate in my superworld. Naturally, though, the same is true for everyone. So it is kind of solipsism for everybody, multi-solipsism! This is what QBism means. As physicist David Mermin states, it is not really solipsism because we coexist, and we communicate:

> QBists are often charged with solipsism: a belief that the world exists only in the mind of a single agent. This is wrong. ... When I converse with you or read your books and articles in *Nature,* I plausibly conclude that you are a perceiving being rather like myself, and infer features of your experience. (2014)

We live in our personal, physical, parallel realities, each one a superworld, but we communicate in the ordinary way.

Vital Information

This multi-solipsism explains a great deal about people and their very different worldviews. Different people have different physical realities. Crucially, this means we have different versions of the probable future for events throughout the whole of the world. No wonder people see things differently. This is one of the huge implications of quantum theory taken at face value. As described in Chapter 15, this view enables us to live in harmony with each other.

The trouble is that although quantum theory has given rise to modern technology that is hugely successful in all kinds of innovative ways, it is almost universally believed that the actual meaning of the science does not really matter to us in our ordinary lives. As physicist Hans von Baeyer writes:

> Flawlessly accounting for the behavior of matter on scales from the subatomic to the astronomical, quantum mechanics is the most successful theory in all the physical sciences. It is also the weirdest. ... Physicists have grappled with the quantum world's apparent paradoxes for nine decades, with little to show for their struggles. The deep confusion about the meaning of quantum theory will continue to add fuel to the perception that the deep things it is so urgently trying to tell us about our world are irrelevant to everyday life and too weird to matter. (2013, 47)

Such perceptions are utterly false as I trust the concepts presented here make clear. The things the science is urgently trying to tell us are certainly very weird but they could not be more relevant.

Firstly, the physical reality actually encountered by each conscious individual is idiosyncratic to that individual. But even that pales beside the inevitable implication. As described in the next chapter, each individual is directly involved with everything that happens in their version of the world. The deep things that quantum theory is trying to tell us include something of extraordinary personal importance to each one of us. We are the unwitting directors of our personal holographic universes with regard to every aspect of the world.

4

Interactive Destiny

Interactive destiny sounds like a contradiction in terms, but this is exactly what happens in the superworld. Unwittingly, one is constantly engaged with the destiny of the whole of one's physical reality.

Destiny

In Newtonian mechanics the world is as predictable as clockwork. We might not know enough about some physical situation that we can predict exactly what will happen in the future, but it is utterly predetermined. In other words, the destiny of the world is fixed and certain. So free will is an illusion, as numerous philosophers have declared.

The new physics shows us something quite different. The state of the world is defined in terms of probabilities, rather than certainties. This means the future is still predetermined, but in terms of probabilities. As each observation is made, the probabilities of future events are changed. So the destiny is constantly changing, as new observations are being made. Still no free will. It all just happens.

The superworld is different again, defined solely by what has been observed. The extraordinary news is that in one's personal world, one is constantly biasing the process of observation, altering the probabilities. As a result one is effectively interacting with the destiny. The origin of this capability is described in Chapter 20, where it is also shown that this means free will becomes a possibility.

Confirmation Bias

The consequences are totally extraordinary but the principle is simple. When experience clashes with expectation, there tends to be a particular type of discomfort. Things aren't right! In psychology this discomfort is called dissonance. Because of this, the unconscious mind will often modify the experience, so as to reduce or eliminate this unpleasant feeling, 'dissonance reduction'. It alters the observation, so it fits better with the expectations, in order to avoid this bad feeling. This is called 'confirmation bias'. The process of observation is biased so that the resulting experience does not jar with the expectations.

It seems obvious, given objective reality, that all this does is produce a rose-tinted view of the world, thinking things turned out how we expected. But in the personal superworld the situation is very different, and the implications of confirmation bias are truly astonishing. It is the biased observation that becomes part of the definition of the physical reality. So rather than just deluding oneself, one is actually doing a jump into a slightly different version of physical reality. If this seems utterly loopy to you, I am right with you. It feels *all* wrong, but it follows directly from standard physics, as described in Appendix IV. The altered observation defines you as existing in a different version of the world in the space of all possible worlds.

A Different Path

As described in Part 2, the basic logic is just like a movie. Each 'frame' of the movie of life is a different holographic universe. The way modern movies work is by adding changes to the existing frame to make the next frame. The holographic universe works in a logically identical manner. As each observation is made, the holographic universe changes to a new version, and this is the next frame. So when bias confirmation causes you to make a different version of an observation, you wind up in a different version of the holographic universe than you otherwise would have.

There is no change to physical reality. All possible versions of physical reality exist in the many-worlds universe. So at every moment, every possible version of the future exists. When confirmation bias causes you to make a different version of an observation, you wind up in a different version of the next frame than you otherwise would have, a different version of the holographic universe. And *this* means that you wind up in a different variation of physical reality as a result. The meaning is extraordinary. This is the version in which the event portrayed by the biased observation did just actually happen. This is what changes the destiny. When the observation is altered, and you wind up in a different version of reality, you are taking a different path into the future through the endlessly branching possibilities. This is described in detail in Chapter 28.

Creative Visualisation

It means you are constantly interacting with the destiny of the whole of your physical reality. This is what makes you the unwitting director. The effect is gradual and holistic, but it is both constant and self-reinforcing. So this is clearly very important to know about. First off this means that positive thinking is vital, kind of Reality Health & Safety. Given this strange empowerment we do not want to encourage unwelcome events. But the really big news lies in the extraordinary effectiveness of 'creative visualisation'. This means using the imagination to picture events that one wants to experience happening in the real world. It works because repeatedly bringing this imagery to mind produces increasing expectation, a well-known psychological phenomenon. The result is that confirmation bias becomes more and more likely. All straightforward standard psychology, but in the personal world the implications are amazing. By building expectations, you make it more likely you will experience them coming true. So creative visualisation means interacting with destiny deliberately.

5

Providence

Research shows that images held in the mind can directly affect what is observed. As neuroscience writer Mo Constandi reports:

> A new study now shows that visual working memory can influence our perceptions, so that mental images in the mind's eye can alter the way we see things. (2011)

So you tend to see in the world what is in your mind's eye, a perfect example of confirmation bias. Visualisation is the deliberate production of mental images in the mind's eye, and repeated visualisation reinforces the mental habituation and thus promotes confirmation bias. This is why creative visualisation works unreasonably well.

Attractors

There is a popular idea called the 'law of attraction', that if you think about the things you want they will be attracted to you. Obviously though, just having certain thoughts does not alter objective physical reality one jot. That is just basic physics. But if you visualise a desired objective consistently and clearly, this will induce expectations, which gives rise to confirmation bias, and this alters the path you take through the branching possibilities. So the effect actually works, but not because anything is attracted *to* you. It seems as if it changes the real world but actually it just changes you, and that changes which version of the world you are likely to gravitate toward in the future.

So repeatedly focusing on the things you want in your life means you are more and more likely to experience them coming true. Technically, the result is a 'strange attractor', meaning an emergent tendency in your holographic universe, as described in Appendix V. What is extraordinary is that this phenomenon applies to the whole of your world. In other words, it affects which version of events you are likely to experience with regard to all events, everywhere. If you had misheard someone saying the result of a major election, you might now be living a version of the world with a different result. That is the extraordinary difference between the reality of a holographic universe and the reality of an ordinary physical world.

It means that positive expectations are very important with regard to *all* of reality. Interactive destiny is a global holistic effect. The positive results of strange attractors is nicely illustrated by the famous mountaineer William Murray:

> ... the moment one definitely commits oneself, then Providence moves too. ... A whole stream of events issues from the decision, raising in one's favor all manner of unforeseen incidents and meetings and material assistance, which no man could have dreamed would have come his way. (1951)

This Providence is the strange attractors in action. When such a commitment is made to an outcome it becomes increasingly anticipated, and thus the expectations create strange attractors. And so it becomes more and more likely to be experienced happening in the real world. Thus in time, as he describes, all kinds of assistance quite outside of ordinary likelihood tend to appear. It seems exactly as if the universe provides assistance. This is interactive destiny at work.

The meaning is fantastic. We can do interactive destiny deliberately, by visualising our desired outcomes and anchoring them in committent. So life really is a game, and a game of skill at that. The rules of play are addressed in Chapter 13. 'Karma' is involved.

6

The World Hologram

For all this to really make sense we need to fully understand the nature of the reality one actually experiences *directly*, the 'perceptual reality', meaning your perception of the world. This is the representation of reality that is generated by the brain, using all the information from the senses of the body. We now know exactly what the perceptual reality is, though this may be unfamiliar. The brain produces a representation of the three-dimensional real world, in the form of a three-dimensional virtual reality, as symbolised in Figure 6.1. As the biologist Richard Dawkins states in *Unweaving the Rainbow*:

> Our brain constructs a three-dimensional model. It is a virtual reality in the head. (1998, 276)

Figure 6.1 The perceptual reality, a three-dimensional model of the world.

Virtual Reality

The brain creates a virtual-reality rendering of reality 'in here' representing the real world 'out there'. This is the brain's navigation system – how one can be aware of the world, and interact with it. This virtual-reality process operates in just the same way as the imagination. The imagination is the faculty of the brain that constructs images of things within the mind, virtual-reality representations of things which are not actually present in reality. The same mechanism is the basis of how human perception actually operates. This is a virtual-reality representation of things which the senses report *are* there and present in reality. As physicist David Deutsch explains:

> Imagination is a straightforward form of virtual reality. What may not be so obvious is that our 'direct' experience of the world through our senses is virtual reality too. ... What we experience directly is a virtual-reality rendering, conveniently generated for us by our unconscious minds from sensory data. (1997, 120)

In other words, what seems to be the direct experience of objective reality 'out there' is in fact the experience of a virtual reality 'in here'. So what is actually experienced *directly* is the virtual-reality rendering of what physical reality looks like, not the physical reality itself.

The Known World

This virtual reality includes not only the representation of what you are experiencing at the moment, but also the experiences of the past, and the layout of the whole world that all this represents. This is your perceptual reality as a whole. This is your entire concept of the world. Whenever you think about any aspect of the world, where you went yesterday, what might be happening now far away, what you are actually experiencing is in fact, of course, this virtual reality.

This includes all the different ways you experience things, and it represents absolutely everything you experience and everything you know. As Deutsch goes on:

> Every last scrap of our external experience is of virtual reality. And every last scrap of our knowledge — including our knowledge of the non-physical worlds of logic, mathematics and philosophy, and of imagination, fiction, art and fantasy — is encoded in the form of programs for the rendering of those worlds on our brain's own virtual-reality generator. (1997, 121)

This is the known world. This is the totality of everything you know about the world, and your concept of reality as a whole.

Projection

There is one more fascinating and vital fact about this virtual reality. It seems totally obvious that what one is experiencing directly is 'out there'. In one sense this is as true as it is obvious, but in another sense it is quite false. As Deutsch explains:

> Consider the nerve signals reaching our brains from our sense organs. Far from providing direct or untainted access to reality, even they themselves are never experienced for what they really are – namely crackles of electrical activity. Nor, for the most part, do we experience them as being *where* they really are – inside our brains. Instead, we place them in the reality beyond. We do not just see blue: we see a blue sky up there, far away. We do not just feel pain: we experience a headache, or a stomach ache. The brain attaches those interpretations – 'head', 'stomach' and 'up there' – to events that are in fact within the brain itself. (2011, 10)

In other words, although the virtual reality itself is going on 'in here' within the brain, it is experienced *as* going on 'out there' in the world, or elsewhere in the body. It is mentally projected out onto the world 'out there'. And this is why we do not notice that what we are actually experiencing directly is a virtual reality 'in here'. But it is. It works so perfectly, corresponding precisely to the world, one can never notice.

The virtual reality being experienced is just like a hologram. It is a spatially-distributed, three-dimensional image that is mentally projected onto the real world, so as to match up precisely. I call it the 'world hologram'. As symbolised in Figure 6.2, it is actually 'in here', but it is experienced as 'out there'.

Figure 6.2 Projection of the world hologram onto reality.

So the reality I am experiencing *directly* is simply the world hologram, a field of information. This is my head-up display of what reality looks like here and now, projected onto the real physical world. And beyond what I can immediately see, this 'fills in' the rest of the world known from all my previous observations. All that is of course imagination, though we do not usually think of it like that.

This world hologram is the display of the human navigation system at work, the 'sensorium'. Remarkably, however, this is also a structure of information of extraordinary significance in the field of physics. As held by various interpretations, this structure of information is what defines the determinacy of the real world encountered. Thus it is determinate only where defined by the world hologram. This is the reason the superworld is a holographic universe. It is that simple. So we have known about the true nature of reality for some time but it has been just too unbelievable.

7

The Inside View

It is well known in physics that there are two very different types of frame of reference involved in the science, but the full significance has remained invisible. It means that the objective reality and the subjective reality are two quite different types of *physical* reality.

Two Views

As Tegmark states, the new physics has taught us that we must carefully distinguish between the two perspectives:

> ... the outside view of a physicist studying its mathematical equations, like a bird surveying a landscape from high above it, and the inside view of an observer living in the world described by the equations, like a frog living in the landscape surveyed by the bird. (2010, 10)

The outside view is the standard objective view. It is simply what physical reality must be like, given the equations of physics. The equations define a quasi-classical world. This is the generally accepted definition of the world, the modern scientific worldview.

The inside view is the subjective reality of a conscious individual actually in the world. This is the perceptual reality, the world hologram. Because it is subjective, this not attributed core relevance in physics. But this omission is what has led to the great paradoxes because physical reality itself is different on outside and inside views.

The Holographic Universe

As Tegmark describes, there are lots of identical copies of you. As Deutsch says, given that there all these identical copies of oneself:

> ... which one am I? I am, of course, all of them. Each of them has just asked that question, 'which one am I?', and any true way of answering that question must give each one of them the same answer. (1997, 279)

The key point here is that they all have identically the same world hologram, otherwise they would not be identically the same person. And as these are all in the same place at the same time, this adds up to a single world hologram. Identical and coincident copies of a structure of information cannot be other than a single instance. Put a dozen identical slides of a graph on an overhead projector and you get just the one graph. The superposition sums to one structure of information. Naturally, the same is true of the world hologram.

This means that *on* this inside view, in the reality of this single world hologram, the physical reality is the reality of all these worlds, all at once, superposed. In other words, on this view the physical reality is a superworld. This is a tautology, an inevitable consequence.

This is how the superworld comes to exist. And as has been described, this means that only what has been observed is determinate, as in QBism. The QBism world is the superworld, the inside-view reality. As it is defined only by observations, the superworld is defined only on the observed surface, and this is the outer boundary of the known world. In other words, this is the holographic universe. It tends to be thought of as a weird spherical shell at the outer edge of the entire cosmos, but it is actually just the world you see. This is the world of the individual on the inside view. As described in the next chapter, this individual is who you really are. The term individual is always used here to mean this entity, the individual 'in here'. The term observer is used exclusively to mean the physical body.

8

The Real Person

Who am I really? My natural idea of myself is that I am a physical being, all too obviously when I have just banged my shin. But sometimes I seem more to be the one living inside my body, as when it has the flu and I am waiting for it to get better. On the inside view this is essentially the case because absolutely everything that defines you as you is defined in your world hologram.

The Indeterminate Body

It seems obvious that the world hologram is defined by the body in which it is instantiated. This of course is exactly the case on the outside view. But on the inside view, in the superworld, even the body is determinate only where observed.

All the things you have observed, your facial structure and so on, are determinate because all the worlds in the superworld are identical with respect to what you have seen. So all these aspects of your body are determinate, like the body of the butterfly. But everything else, like the positions of small internal blood vessels, is the sum of all the different versions of how that part of the body could be, like the wings of the butterfly. Thus even your own body is only determinate where defined by the observations. In other words, it is indeterminate except where defined by the world hologram. This forms the 'self-avatar'.

The Self-Avatar

On the outside view, each version of your body, living in one of these worlds, is a real ordinary determinate body, with blood pumping through the network of blood vessels, all of which have specific and determinate arrangements. But on the inside view your body is only real and determinate where you have directly observed it.

So what am I exactly? I am the world hologram. This does not seem much the usual idea of personal identity, the whole physical being, but in fact it defines exactly the identity I am used to.

At the centre of the world hologram is the 'self-avatar'. This is the complete mental image of myself, built up from all the observations of myself, looking in the mirror, hearing what people say I am like, and so on. This is what I know myself to be, as a physical entity, as a person, as a participant in society and so on. This is the full self-identity, my complete conception of myself.

Just as the actual form of the perceptual reality is not generally seen for exactly what it is, the form of the self-avatar is not generally recognised either. This is the three-dimensional representation of the whole of me. Just as the world hologram represents the three-dimensional physical reality of the world, the avatar at the centre represents the three-dimensional physical reality of me. And the body is determinate only where defined by this self-avatar.

The self-avatar figure is of course just a structure of information in the brain. But as Deutsch explains, quoted back on page 25, it is not experienced like that. It is mentally projected and perfectly mapped onto the physical body, just like the rest of the world hologram is with the world. And *this* is what is directly experienced. Even when you look in the mirror, what you are experiencing *directly* is the self-avatar figure, the representation of the physical body in the world hologram, just as Deutsch describes. By definition it is just a structure of information in the brain, but you experience it *as* the real you, solid and actual, in the middle of your reality.

The True Self

Obviously, the self-avatar figure is literally just a conceptualisation, a mental representation of who and what you know yourself to be. It is literally who you know yourself to be. And yet, it is this field of information that defines everything determinate about you in the personal superworld in which you live. As described in Chapter 12, this is the complete definition of the 'functional identity', everything that makes you who you are. Your self-avatar figure is the complete and total definition of your mental and physical presence. The rest of the world hologram is your unconscious as described in Chapter 15.

This is just the effect. Nothing is lost. You are a physical entity, but your body is the superposed sum of all those bodies in which you exist. In the world you encounter directly the net result is determinate only where observed. The self-avatar is the whole of the definition of who you actually are, physically, in reality, on the inside view. Strangely, therefore, not to mention ironic, you are exactly who you know yourself to be. You *are* the world hologram. You *have* a body.

This leaves one major question unanswered. All this has been a description of the reality of the inside view, but *whose* view is this exactly? The world hologram is the perceptual reality, and this is the information that is being perceived. This is what *gets* experienced. Who is *doing* the experiencing? The world hologram cannot be both the entity being perceived, and also doing the perceiving at the same time. That is like trying to lift yourself up by your own bootstraps. The answer to this conundrum is consciousness. This is the other key attribute of your true self.

This is using the word consciousness in a very specific way, as will be fully explained in Chapter 10. In order to get to the extraordinary significance of this consciousness in a scientific and logical manner, we first need to address the great paradox of relativity. This is the subject of the next chapter.

9

Time

Relativity is universally acknowledged as the correct description of the nature of the world, but great paradoxes are present here also. The physics tells us without question that time is a linear dimension, just like the three dimensions of space. And this means that the past and even the future exist in the same way as the North and the South. In other words, the whole vast span of time exists 'already'. This is a four-dimensional space-time 'block universe'. The problem is this means there can be no such thing as the passage of time.

Although this was taken as obvious fact by Einstein, it is still the subject of heated argument in philosophy, but there is a yet more fundamental paradox. As he stated very clearly, physics cannot define the phenomenon of the present moment, 'the Now' as he called it. Clearly something of central significance is missing. All this is described in technical detail in Chapters 18 and 19.

The Moving Viewpoint

The terse canonical statement of physicist Hermann Weyl solves both these problems at a stroke. As he emphasises:

> The objective world simply *is*, it does not *happen*. Only to the gaze of my consciousness, crawling upward along the life-line of my body, does a section of this world come to life as a fleeting image in space which continuously changes in time. (1949, 116)

This life-line is now known as the 'worldline', meaning the line one traces through the four-dimensional space-time of the world. Figure 9 symbolises a sequence of moments in my life, working on the book. So this represents a little segment of my worldline. Each two-dimensional picture represents the three-dimensional physical reality in a specific state, at a specific moment in time. As the experiencing consciousness sweeps through these moments, up the worldline of the body, there is the experience of reality, moment after moment, being me, working on my computer. Consequently, there is the *effect* of time passing, as moment after moment is experienced. This is how consciousness gives rise to the experience of the passage of time. This is what Weyl is describing.

When you take a train journey, it is clear that you are passing through the landscape of the track. Obviously, the landscape is not moving. It is just your view *of* the landscape that is changing. But inside the train, from your moving viewpoint, you experience the passage of the landscape. Weyl is saying that the experience of the passage of time is exactly the same kind of thing. The world simply is. It does not change at all. What is changing is the perspective of the moving viewpoint. As the moving viewpoint of consciousness, the Now, passes along the track of the worldline, into the future in the space-time layout, there is the effect of the passage of time.

Figure 9 Segment of a worldline.

10

Consciousness

Weyl's elegant solution to the paradoxes obviously makes sense. Clearly, inevitably, since one is constantly experiencing the sequence of moments in life, as we all do, the viewpoint of consciousness is moving through the moments. The problem is this means consciousness cannot be a physical phenomenon, but something quite different. It has to be to physical reality as the train is to the landscape it passes through. This is automatically rejected in modern physics because 'physicalism' is taken for granted, meaning that nothing exists that is not physical or caused by the physical. But as Weyl makes clear, this consciousness is not an attribute of the physical world:

> ... the consciousness in this function does not belong to the world. (1934, 1)

Two Phenomena

It is important to understand that Weyl is using the word consciousness in a very specific way. The word consciousness is indiscriminately used for two very different kinds of phenomena, and the result is a big muddle. This is explained in detail by philosopher of consciousness David Chalmers. As he describes in his book *The Conscious Mind* (1996) the word consciousness is used both for that which *gets* experienced, which is of course a property of the brain, and the *experiencing*, which is not. The distinction is vital because without it the whole subject of consciousness never really makes sense.

That which gets experienced he calls the 'psychological consciousness'. This is essentially the information processing capability of the organism that produces the perceptual reality, the world hologram, with all the attendant faculties of cognition that arise as a result. This is now well understood in a practical manner in the field of neuroscience. But the experiencing itself is something completely different. This he calls the 'phenomenal consciousness'. This is the experiencing *of* this field of information. There is no known explanation for this phenomenon in modern science. Here, the word consciousness on its own is used exclusively to mean this experiencing consciousness.

The Hard Problem

There has been tremendous difficulty in even describing this consciousness. Its existence has even been denied, hard as that is to comprehend, but it is of course utterly real. As Chalmers emphasises:

> When we think and perceive, there is a whir of information-processing, but there is also a subjective aspect. As Nagel (1974) has put it, there is *something it is like* to be a conscious organism. This subjective aspect is experience. When we see, for example, we *experience* visual sensations. (1995)

The phenomenon is utterly fundamental, but finding an explanation for it, or even framing the problem clearly, is what Chalmers calls the hard problem of consciousness. Without question this phenomenon is totally inexplicable by anything in the physical world. As noted by philosopher of mind Jerry Fodor:

> Nobody has the slightest idea how anything material could be conscious. So much for our philosophy of consciousness. (1992)

The answer is simple. It cannot. It is not of the world. The great physicist Erwin Schrödinger took the same view as Weyl:

> Consciousness cannot be accounted for in physical terms. For consciousness is absolutely fundamental. It cannot be accounted for in terms of anything else. (1931)

This is what Chalmers demonstrates in his book. As he proposes, the experiencing itself should be taken as:

> ... a fundamental feature of the world, alongside mass, charge, and space-time. (1995, 216)

> ... experience must be taken as something over and above the physical properties of the world. (1996, 331)

In other words, consciousness is contextual to reality, on a par with space-time, the entirety of existence. It is universe consciousness.

The Point of View

Of course, consciousness seems all too obviously to be just something happening in the brain. Clearly, 'in here' is where all the experiencing is going on. And this of course is what gives the impression that *all* consciousness is a brain thing, both psychological and phenomenal. But this is just how a virtual reality works. It is experienced from the inside, but the ultimate *experiencer*, in digital video games the player, is not actually inside the virtual reality.

When you take a picture of the scenery, this records the view from a specific position, a point in space. This is the viewpoint of the visual perspective. Just like any camera picture, any virtual reality has a specific point of view, meaning the virtual reality is formulated with respect to a specific point in the space, like Google Earth. Rotate the point of view and you see it in a different direction. Move the point of view and you see it from a different location.

The virtual reality of the world hologram is formulated with respect to the standard human viewpoint, which is 'in here' behind the eyes. As this is where reality is experienced *from,* it seems totally obvious this is where the experiencing consciousness *is*. But just as you are not really there in Google Earth, or up in the air when piloting a flight simulator, the experiencing consciousness is not in the brain. It is an utterly different type of phenomenon.

Consciousness is Primary

Given the ever-moving present moment as an obvious and indisputable fact, it is clear that Weyl must be right. But this means that something that cannot be explained by the physical world, the consciousness, is indeed fundamental. This is almost universally dismissed as nonsense nowadays in modern physics, but this was not always so. As stated by the physicist Max Planck, who discovered quanta, receiving the Nobel Prize in 1919:

> I regard consciousness as fundamental. I regard matter as derivative from consciousness. We cannot get behind consciousness. Everything that we talk about, everything that we regard as existing, postulates consciousness. (1931)

The idea that consciousness should be relevant to how the world works is usually rejected automatically but this is what fits the facts. As stated by Michel Bitbol, Director of Research in Applied Epistemology[1] at the French National Centre for Scientific Research:

> Consciousness is *existentially*, *transcendentally*, and *methodologically* primary. (2008, 16)

However disparaged it may now be, taking consciousness as fundamental makes complete sense of the paradoxes of relativity.

This also explains the extraordinary status of the inside view, and the central relevance of the world hologram in the new physics. It is this reality that is directly and immediately experienced by universe consciousness. This also makes clear that the phenomenon of the superworld is inevitable. To consciousness, inherently omnipresent, there can only be one of a specific world hologram. So the physical reality is the superworld of all the worlds that instantiate it.

---

1 Scientific theories seek to explain how systems operating in reality work, in fields such as economics, climatology and physics. Applied epistemology examines the explanation to see if the logic is fully coherent and operational, in other words, to see if the explanation really works.

11

The Philosopher's Stone

Now we come to the other major perk of the new worldview. Given the nature of the individual in quantum theory, plus the nature of consciousness implied by relativity, we are effectively immortal.

Consciousness Continues

In earlier times, before we properly understood the physics of the real world, immortality was simply a matter of faith. But nowadays, given our scientific worldview, it seems obvious it is more a matter of self-delusion. The body dies, so surely the inner life must die too. How could there possibly be any continuation of life after the death of the body? Where would you be? What would you be? As it turns out you would still be you, but just in a different situation. As futurist Hans Moravec states, immortality is just inevitable. When we die:

> We lose our ties to physical reality, but, in the space of all possible worlds, that cannot be the end. Our consciousness continues to exist in some of those, and we will always find ourselves in worlds where we exist and never in ones where we don't. (1998)

Here consciousness means the psychological consciousness, the ongoing process of the world hologram. In the space of all possible worlds, the many-worlds universe, there is inevitably a world in which your world hologram continues. So the experience of death in this world leads straight on to the experience of life in the next world.

Quantum Immortality

Moravec is by no means the only scientist to realise that the many-worlds universe directly implies immortality. As stated by Marcus Chown, cosmology consultant at *New Scientist* magazine:

> If the Many Worlds is correct, it seems the only certainty in life is not death but immortality. We're *all* gonna live forever. (2002, 40)

And the majority of physicists in the directly affected fields of experimental physics now consider the many-worlds theory to be correct. Deutsch simply states this as incontrovertible fact. Here he is using the word universe for what is now called a parallel world:

> The point that theorists tend to miss is that the multiplicity of reality is not only, or even primarily, a consequence of quantum theory. It is quite simply an observed fact. ... So other universes exist in exactly the same sense that the single universe that we see exists. This is not a matter of interpretation. It is a logical consequence of quantum theory, albeit one that somehow, seventy years after the theory was discovered, is still in dispute. (1996)

Many physicists are still reluctant to accept this because it seems so weird, but as explained in Part 2 this is the direct consequence of taking the quantum theory at face value. Deutsch is the founding father of quantum computing. As he explains (Chown, 2001) quantum computers only work because they make use of parallel worlds.

The Moravec Jump

There is one thing missing from the concept of immortality that Moravec describes, namely continuity from one world to the next. Why should experience necessarily continue, jumping from one worldline to another? The nature of the experiencing consciousness provides the answer. Being a property of the universe it does not switch off when you die. It goes on forever, so experience continues straight on to a new version of reality, just as Moravec describes.

You could think of it like the end of Part 1 of a movie that straight-away continues on with Part 2. Consciousness is to the space of all possible worlds as a computer system is to the domain of its memory where movies are stored. The computer can access any place in the memory, and it can jump from one point to any other. It can play Part 1 of a movie from one block of memory, and then continue straight on and play Part 2 of the movie from a different block. Consciousness does exactly the same kind of thing, except that each part of the movie of life is one lifetime in the space of all possible worlds.

So when there is an end to one lifetime, consciousness automatically experiences the lifetime that makes the most natural continuation, wherever that happens to exist in the universe of all possible worlds. It means death is not the end. It is a jump from this lifetime, on this physical worldline, to the next. I call this the 'Moravec jump'. In experience, reality continues forever.

Continuation

Given our current scientific worldview it seems totally obvious that death is the end. Not so, the new physics tells us. This is what we have discovered but not recognised. When you die in this life, you wake up somewhere else. Your experience of reality continues in a different version of reality, one that somehow includes you.

Objectively, this is of course monumentally unlikely, but that does not matter. The likelihood of there being a version of the world that contains the perfect and natural next moment to follow on from the end of your life here is small, very small indeed, but this makes no difference. It could be infinitesimal and it would still work. Given the existence of all possible worlds, this is what consciousness experiences. However fantastically improbable it might be, it actually exists as Moravec states. The quantum definition of the universe includes all possible worlds, and so there is always a reality in which there is an exact continuation of your life, in some world somewhere.

Immortal Beings

On the inside view the movie of life goes on forever. The world hologram lives on. This is certainly a tremendous shift in our understanding of life, but the idea of such a transformation is nothing new. This is the legendary philosopher's stone of alchemy. It is not a magical rock. It is simply the knowledge with which a new concept of life is built. Consciousness continues, and the self 'in here' goes on.

As the psychologist Carl Jung records, the knowledge of immortality makes a huge difference to life:

> ... for most people it means a great deal to assume that their lives will have an indefinite continuity beyond the present existence. They live more sensibly, feel better, and are more at peace. One has centuries, one has an inconceivable period of time at one's disposal. What then is the point of this senseless mad rush? (1963, 4)

The psychological effects of the desperate sense of time pressure can hardly be missed in the modern world. And without question the mad rush may well be construed as the outward visible sign of 'terror management', the coping mechanism of not looking too deeply at the inevitability of impending death and annihilation. To be free of all this obviously frees up a great deal of mental energy.

The true identity on the inside view is the world hologram, experienced by universe consciousness. We are not just physical beings that happen to be having experiences. We are primarily beings of experience that happen to be experiencing a particular lifetime at the moment, in a particular physical body. Once we know that we are world holograms, and consciousness is unending, it is clear that the experience of life inevitably continues, just as Moravec declares. This kind of being is naturally immortal because the movie of life runs on from lifetime to lifetime. Death is not annihilation. We need no longer fear being snuffed out. Dying in this lifetime means waking up in the next one. In experience, we are immortal.

12

The Soul

If we are immortal, how come do we not remember any previous lifetimes? Because this is a newbie world. Everyone is a first-timer, born as a baby. In the next lifetime you will find yourself awakening in a new, fully-formed adult body, with all your memories intact. And no belly button. This is far the most likely form of reincarnation.

New Bodies

As Deutsch explains, we will soon have the technology to manufacture complete, functional human bodies:

> Illness and old age are going to be cured soon – certainly within the next few lifetimes ... by creating backups of the states of brains, which could be uploaded into new, blank brains in identical bodies if a person should die. (2011, 455)

This technology of the future is portrayed in the movie *Altered Carbon* where it is called re-sleeving. Taking it one step further, once the technology exists it can also be used to create completely new people.

Whatever happens to our particular version of life on Earth, this has to happen somewhere in the space of all possible worlds. Suppose some society in the future needs a lot of new people right away, complete with adult characters and capabilities. Simple enough with this technology, they just make a lot of new bodies and then initialise each one with the mental capabilities they need. They give each person a character and a history by uploading an adult world hologram into the brain, a record of a lifetime of experiences. Let's say they want a broad spectrum of characters, so they simply generate world holograms of people who could have lived at some time, in a world like theirs. So they are making new bodies, with real pre-existing characters. They are effectively reincarnating old souls.

In the space of all possible worlds, every possible variation of this process must occur. So in some version of the world it is your world hologram, exactly as it is at the moment of your death, that gets used to initialise this brand new body. So you wake up in this new body, next moment after death. Obviously this is science fiction, but it is also just regular science. Without question this is fantastically unlikely, but that makes no odds. It is real because all possibilities exist. So when you die you wake up in some future environment. That is what happens when your consciousness is universe consciousness.

The Functional Identity

It seems strange to think of oneself as just a field of information, a world hologram, but as described in Chapter 8 this is the whole of the real you 'in here'. This is all of your 'functional identity', meaning the operational psychology, what you are like, how you think. It is not only all the memory of one's life that is contained in the virtual reality of the world hologram, but also the way thinks. As Deutsch states:

> All reasoning, all thinking and all external experience are forms of virtual reality. (1997, 121)

So just as all one's knowledge about the world is contained in the world hologram, so too is every aspect of one's character, and how one thinks and makes decisions. This defines all the attributes that define the operational individual in terms of character and memory, thoughts and feelings, experience, beliefs, criteria and values, and the habitual thoughts, behaviours, routines and practices. This is the complete functional identity, meaning the whole of that which makes you who you are. As described in Chapter 8, everything else is indeterminate. This is described in more detail in Chapter 30.

So this is the real you, that which defines what you are really like 'in here', living your life, making decisions and getting things done. As this is the complete functional identity, if just this is reincarnated then the new entity is the whole of you, exactly as you are now 'in here', in the new body.

Reincarnation

The world hologram defines everything about you that is real and determinate. So in every possible way this is your true identity on the inside view. This is the real you. You *are* the world hologram. This may seem very odd, but it is also very good news. It means it really is all of the real you that wakes up in a new body after death. This is what effectively passes from lifetime to lifetime. The world hologram is your immortal soul.

Life after death obviously requires a human body to operate in, well, more or less human anyway. Theoretically the body could be of any sort with the right sort of interface, i.e. a world hologram. It could be like a Na'vi body in the movie *Avatar*, human shape but blue, slender and ten feet tall with a prehensile tail and Spockish ears. That might well not be exactly what you were hoping for, but there is no reason why it should not be anything you can imagine. More likely you would prefer to wake up as you were when you were younger, or some other ideal expression of how you imagine yourself in a perfect world. This is exactly the kind of thing it is useful to focus on as we get older because interactive destiny will operate here also.

As the holographic being you truly are, as the soul, you are immortal. Naturally, such ideas can seem extremely suspect in this modern age. We have largely freed ourselves from dogma and superstition which now look like primitive wishful thinking. But it turns out that certain great myths are grounded in intuitions that have a true basis in reality. Universe consciousness is spirit, a vital, universal, animating principle. And this leads to the immortality of the soul as a natural conclusion. So when the body dies, the being 'in here' passes on. And you awaken in the next life. The timeless wisdom is true.

Exactly what kind of beings we really are has remained quite a mystery in the modern world, largely because in modern science everything is defined solely with respect to physical reality. But as held in the Pagan religions, we are triune, body, soul and spirit. This is explored in more detail in Part 2.

Transmutation

As Jung states, this knowledge makes a tremendous difference to life. This is the philosopher's stone that turns base metal into gold. This mythical transmutation can be seen as a metaphor for the transformation of identity, from the mortal physical body to the immortal world hologram. The term base metal simply means a common and inexpensive metal, as opposed to a precious metal such as gold or silver. The meaning here is that base metals corrode and decay, eventually disappearing altogether, but gold does not corrode. The gold is a metaphor for an eternal entity. This would therefore be the 'opus magnum' of alchemy, literally the great work, the rebirth of the psyche in immortal form.

One of the most significant implications is that this world is effectively a kindergarten world. We are all first-timers, learning the ropes, with many lifetimes to come. The unseen challenge is to learn how to manage our worlds, as discussed in the following chapters. In abandoning the great mythical traditions we have lost sight of the meaning of life and it is immense. The game of life is actually very long-term and big-horizon. In the fullness of time all things are possible. What we may become is unlimited. And with interactive destiny, and all the time in the world, there is everything to play for.

13

Inherent Morality

The implications of interactive destiny give rise to another phenomenon very alien to modern science, the ancient concept of karma. This is a principle of cause and effect in spiritual traditions where the things you do to others in some way 'happen back to you', seemingly out of the blue. Interactive destiny shows us that there is a scientific explanation of why exactly this tends to happen. A strange attractor is generated in your superworld. This is all highly significant because it defines an inherent morality, and this is vital to humanity's success.

Reality Reflects

As you go through life, your world hologram increasingly contains observations of the kinds of actions you perform, and thus the kinds of events you yourself are bringing about. Of course, in the logic of the ordinary world, one would not generally expect these kinds of events to be those that would necessarily happen to oneself. Unless one believes that God might take a hand: "Vengeance is mine; I will repay sayeth the Lord." (Romans 12:19; KJV). But in the ordinary physical world there can be no such phenomenon. In the superworld, however, this is just the sort of thing that tends to happen.

These observations form fundamental data about what happens in this reality. This world is therefore defined as one in which actions of this nature are happening. So they become increasingly powerful *unconscious* expectations. And this means that confirmation bias operates just as effectively, if not more so. The result is a strange attractor, meaning an emergent tendency in your holographic universe. The unconscious expectations bias which way the path of your reality goes, just as conscious ones do. Thus your future more and more defines a world in such things tend to happen. So over time, the events in the reality of your superworld more and more reflect the things that you do. Inevitably therefore, sooner or later, these kinds of events are likely to start happening to you as well. Karma operates.

It is important to understand this is not the vengeance of God, or the judgement of the universe. This is just how reality operates, as mainstream Buddhism has always held. This is simply the unconscious operation of interactive destiny. It is all down to oneself.

Heaven and Hell

It seems all too obvious that people get away with doing bad things, but the tendencies of karma may build up very gradually. And this means that the whole thing is off the scope of our normal radar because it is far too long-term. Even looking at life long-term, though, there seems little evidence for karma in our everyday world. The news tells of many who do harm to others and seem to get away with it indefinitely. True, but this is like Road Runner running off a cliff and staying up ... momentarily. Any outstanding balance of karma is reckoned in full at the end of the life. That is the really scary thing about death. The full force of karma happens in the transition from this lifetime to the next. All of the karma takes effect, all at once.

The world we are living in now is mostly very stable, but the opposite applies in the Moravec jump. Absolutely anything could be reality in the next lifetime. The only certainty is your world hologram. The version of the world you find yourself in, out of all possible worlds, will be the one with the best fit with your world hologram. In other words, all the tendencies in reality defined by your world hologram, the karma, will be perfectly expressed in the way this world works, and the kinds of things that are likely to happen. It could be a heaven or a hell. It all depends on the things one has done. This means there really is an inherent morality. But this has none of the connotations of 'moral absolutism', an objective standard handed down from on high. It is just a fundamental operational principle of a personal, holographic universe, defined by your observations.

High and Low

The question of morality has been heavily debated ever since there have been philosophers – always. The legendary naturalist Charles Darwin (1981, 122) provides us with a scientific view. We are naturally empathic beings, social animals capable of understanding others as beings like ourselves. This is the basis of the great success of our race. He divided the effects of morality into altruism and selfishness, which he called the high moral rules and the low moral rules. The high moral rules are based on the impulse to benefit others, even if this is not to one's own advantage. The low moral rules are the set of rational principles that one knows from education and experience one is required to conform to, in order to get by in society.

Karma means that the things you do tend to happen back to you, so there is a basic, selfish motivation to help others prosper, or at least not to disadvantage or harm. So a humanitarian principle is built in. Given karma, the high moral rules become the only rational way of life because living at the expense of others is directly counter to one's own best interests. In other words, the high moral rules are the basic principles of Reality Health & Safety in a superworld. In this kind of reality egoism is potentially disastrous. That is literally the road to hell. Ignoring and trampling over the needs and well-being of others is clocking up bad karma, and it all takes effect in the blink of an eye, in the transition to the next lifetime. In this light it becomes clear that ignoring the high moral rules is deeply damaging to one's future. A transformation of my egoistic agenda begins.

The User Manual

The Noble Eightfold Path of Buddhism is the user manual for this kind of reality, the operating instructions for a holographic universe. This is simply the behavioural definition of how to generate only positive strange attractors. Right Action, firstly doing no harm, is the simplest and most powerful way to live life so that things tend to flow in one's favour. This is the path to good karma, interacting with destiny for nothing but good. This produces an increasingly fortunate life as one makes one's way through the infinite possibilities.

The famous Ten Commandments provide the quick-start guide. This is the vital "Do Not!" list – because if you do these things they will tend to happen more and more in your life. It is like driving on the wrong side of the road. You might get away with it for a while but there is bound to be a hideous conclusion. As sages have been trying to tell us for some time, ignoring the great spiritual principles is perilous.

Behind the dogma lies the idea of positive intent to all. If God is love, then the first commandment means to take love as your only God. And in this kind of reality that is exactly what works, intending and doing only good. This is the cardinal rule for individuals in their own lives, and also for whole cultures and societies. In a primitive culture, cooperation and mutual support are naturally required for success in the close-knit group, giving rise to the cohesion essential for survival. Then, as large, diverse, social structures developed in the world of civilisation and science, religion took up this imperative of the high moral rules, 'agape', the ideal of unconditional selfless love, for many centuries. But this has now been largely abandoned, even by many who self-identify as religious. We now need to reinvigorate this imperative or perish by our own hand, as described in the next chapter. As stated by von Baeyer, there are deep things that the new physics is urgently trying to tell us. The inherent morality is one of them, perhaps the most important of all. It is now a pressing necessity for the survival and success of our human race.

14

Survival

Clearly, the new worldview is of tremendous importance in our personal lives. Awareness of interactive destiny makes us much more able to live successfully in every way. But we are urgently in need of a way to live *together* more successfully on our spaceship Earth. Here it is proposed that the new worldview has the potential to resolve the terrible ills of our modern global culture.

The Solution

There are a number of think tanks assembled to consider 'global catastrophic risks', meaning disasters that threaten the survival of our human race. There are two categories, human caused and external, with ten or so major risks in each. The human ones are all relatively short term, and none are being well managed. As John Holdren, scientific adviser to President Obama, reports on climate change:

> The current situation of the world ... is that we are in a car with bad brakes driving toward the edge of a cliff in the fog ... prudence requires that we try to stop the car. (Friedman, 2008, 160)

Because these problems are all self-induced, there is just one type of solution that resolves them all and will also stand the test of time. In other words, this transforms the chances of our survival as a race. As stated by Alexander King, the pioneering environmentalist who co-founded the Club of Rome, a longstanding think tank:

> Any durable solution to [humanity's] external and internal problems can only come from evolution beyond the egoism that motivates every individual. The wisdom we desperately require can only come through inner transformation. ... This seems the only hope of breaking the impasse of both great danger and great promise, in which mankind is presently constrained. (2006, 22)

The new worldview brings about exactly the change King describes. Given the inherent morality, egoism is always ultimately disastrous for the person. So the only sane and sensible approach to life is taking the other people in the world into account, at least in principle. The fundamental imperative to agape of the great religions is reborn. This leads to 'enlightened self-interest', acting to the benefit of others in order to serve one's own self-interest – doing well by doing good.

The egoism rampant in the modern world is the specific cause of the ruination of our ecosphere. As environmental advocate Speth describes, quoted in the Preface, the top environmental problems are selfishness, greed and apathy, and this is pretty much the definition of egoism in action. This is what it looks like in terms of behaviour. And in our current materialistic culture such conduct seems perfectly natural. But with the new worldview, the rational ground itself is shifted because standard egoism is no longer basic common sense but the very opposite.

In the light of the new worldview karma is a real phenomenon. Every harmful action breeds a potential damage. But every good deed done improves both this life and the next. Understanding this means that the very basis of egoism is redefined. In principle, I want to do good because the way I treat the world is the way the world treats me. Thus while the same basic egoism operates, there is a different and much wider agenda. I want to be sure my actions do only good by everyone, not just for myself. This is still a purely selfish motivation, but it achieves exactly the effect the human race is so desperately in need of. This seeds the vital change in our human nature. It means that enlightened self-interest becomes the only rational perspective. The seeds of a moral modern culture are sown.

The Ideal

A wonderful idea, but worldwide adoption of an altruistic transformation seems a tad unlikely. But the great thing is to have a vision. This at least gives the ideal world some form. And this is exactly what we have been missing, to our great loss. The world is rife with disaster movies but the ideal world for everyone is rarely portrayed.

This is one of the great strengths of traditional religions, an expectation of the ideal. This type of vision for an ideal future is no longer seen as credible by many in the modern world, but the baby is gone with the bathwater and for so many life seems inherently pointless. In all seriousness, the human race at large exbibits the key indicator of clinical depression – being incapable of formulating a positive future.

This is desperately important because this is directing which way our global culture actually goes. This is the kind of thing leading journalist Thomas Friedman (2016, 13) calls steering 'the Machine', meaning the gears and pulleys of the world's biggest forces shaping events. The great majority of people connected to the modern media culture are being exposed to gross negative depictions, and thus our expectations are becoming abysmal. Horrifyingly, but inevitably, much of it is real news, which is then aped in every kind of fiction.

Unwittingly, we have been steering the Machine over a precipice. Instead we need to envision the ideal. The mind has to have something to aim for, a picture of a wonderful future to adopt. At the personal level this generates positive strange attractors, and life gets better. And the more it catches on, the more the global human culture is transformed. The new worldview heals by reconnecting us with reality, who we really are, and how reality actually works. This is the original principle of religion in the full and proper sense of the word. In Latin religare means reconnection. This is connecting with the true identity. As such you are at cause in the superworld, thus you are empowered to make a difference as well as being responsible. The potential for positive and extraordinary change is open-ended.

15

The Higher Self

With modern science we have produced a global interconnected culture and taken over the planet, a remarkable evolution in terms of our capabilities. But a very different type of evolution is the next step for humanity. As we soon learn in childhood, we are insignificant specks in the grand scheme of things, but the full truth is very different. We are world holograms, and the world hologram defines the determinacy of the holographic universe in which one lives. One is not aware of this because this is the unconscious. This is all part of the much greater identity of the individual, the 'higher self', from which most of us are deeply estranged. The next great step of evolution is the realisation of this level of identity, with all its powerful implications.

Macrocosm and Microcosm

'Macrocosm and Microcosm', or 'As Above So Below', is the mythical idea that the world reflects the individual nature, and vice versa. There is a deep correlation between human being and cosmos. This concept is found throughout the history of thought over millennia, and it is part of traditional Buddhism. Clearly this seems like total nonsense in light of the modern scientific worldview. But when the macrocosm is the superworld the myth is simply correct. The Above and the Below are both defined completely by the world hologram. In the ancient literature the Above is the cosmos, and this means the order and the arrangement of the world. As we have seen, the determinacy of the superworld is defined entirely by the world hologram. For each individual, the cosmos is the holographic universe of the superworld.

This confirms another seemingly radical myth. As the modern sage Krishnamurti states:

> You and the world are not two different entities. You 'are' the world, not as an ideal, but actually. (Lutyens, 1983, 74)

With our current worldview we are probably inclined to think he is talking about some cosmic experience of connection which is quite outside ordinary rational everyday life, but the new physics shows us this is literally the case. As Schrödinger stated, quoting the Vedas of ancient Hindu literature: "*I am the entire world*" (Moore, 1989).

It does not feel like that, of course, but this is because we are so divorced from the unconscious. As described in Chapter 30, the world hologram is the 'personal unconscious'. This is the major part of the psyche of the individual. This is where the intuitions we have about how to proceed in life come from. Now we discover that this also defines the determinacy of the whole of the real world. It is in this sense that you are the entire world.

The customary definition of the higher self is an eternal, omnipotent, conscious, and intelligent being who is one's real self. This sounds pretty grand, but the full nature of each conscious individual is quite a bit like this. The reality is that you are not only immortal and at cause, but you also define your world. Not exactly omnipotent though.

This is a big help in making sense of interactive destiny. You are in a truly extraordinary relationship to the world compared to our accustomed view. Not only are you the world in terms of definition, you are also the pilot of your physical reality. Like steering a supertanker, there is a huge inertia, so it changes direction very slowly. The trick is to use the 'trim tab'. The trim tab is a mini-rudder on the back of the rudder that is much easier to move. This turns the rudder, and the rudder turns the ship. Creative visualisation is the trim tab of the holographic universe.

Transformation

As a result of this extraordinary relationship to the world there is a remarkable empowerment. As Krishnamurti goes on to say:

> As the world is yourself, in the transformation of yourself you produce a transformation in society. (Lutyens, 1983, 74)

This is not because your extraordinary example causes others to follow your lead, unless of course you have qualities like Mahatma Gandhi. It is just that when you live in accordance with the principles of Right Action, doing no harm, expecting a better version of the world, you are biasing the path of your world toward the good. For an individual with this self-identity, the full responsibility of one's place in life is realised. This is a key property of the higher self. One is at cause. And the interaction with destiny arising from every action and every thought is increasingly acknowledged. This vision of the ideal future persistently steers toward a better world.

This is essential for us to understand if our race is to survive the near future, and the consequences of ever more powerful technology wielded by single individuals. We need to create a cooperative, altruistic, global society, the culture of the higher self. This is the solution to the predicament of our race, a path of evolution leading not just to survival but onward to the fulfilment of the tremendous potential for our success. We now need to take the new physics at face value and acknowledge not only the unique significance of the individual but also the responsibility. We need to take on the meaning of what we have discovered, how reality actually works and who we really are. It is not just that we live in physical realities that are very different to what we thought. We actually live in different worlds to each other, each one a holographic universe. And we are these worlds. A new culture of respect and right action based on these understandings opens up the possibility of a new age of global human success. This is the next great step in human evolution.

16

Conclusion to Part 1

The next great step in human evolution is not a physical development but a new intelligence, an upgrade for the obsolete egoistic, combative software of the human mind. This is the effect of understanding the extraordinary nature of the real world, and the immediacy of the relationship one has with it all. Given that you are experiencing the passage of time and events happening, your consciousness is universe consciousness. Your identity is the world hologram, which is your eternal soul. The body is your physical vehicle, your incarnation. You are triune, spirit, soul and body. Your world is a holographic universe defined solely by the observations forming the world hologram.

In the light of the inherent morality the only intelligent approach to life is to do one's best to live in harmony with everybody. Generally adopted, this induces a sea change in the interconnected human culture, giving rise to a cohesive global society. A new age is born.

The New Worldview

The eminent theoretical physicist John Wheeler proposed that:

> ... reality grows out of the act of observation, and thus consciousness itself: it is "participatory". (Meijer, 2015, Abstract)

Interactive destiny means our observations are participatory in a whole new dimension. One is directly taking part in which version of the events of the world one is likely to encounter. This is the connection to nature we have been so desperately lacking, a very different kind of relationship. Now it is time for us to take on the full implications of the extraordinary discoveries of the new physics that have passed unrecognised. Interactive destiny, karma and immortality are real phenomena in the superworld of each individual. Naturally, no such things exist, or are possible, in objective physical reality. This is the nature of an entirely different type of domain, the personal holographic universe defined by the superworld.

It all seems too fantastic, but once the impossible is eliminated, whatever remains, no matter how improbable it may seem, has to be the explanation. That is standard science and everyday engineering.

In quantum theory this means the world is personal, as described in QBism. This in turn means interactive destiny. One is constantly piloting the path of reality. So we are the directors of our holographic universes. It also means karma and the inherent morality. Taking more than one gives not only constantly downgrades this life, it literally makes a hell of the next. Living generously makes both better. Lacking these understandings we have been pilots asleep at the wheel.

In relativity this means that consciousness is universe consciousness, as leading physicists have intimated. This in turn implies immortality because consciousness always continues to experience. As Jung states, quoted in Chapter 11, this understanding is highly beneficial to the human psyche. The knowledge of an indefinite continuity makes available a wonderful inner peace. There is all the time in the world, literally. And thus balance is naturally restored between the special value of the present moment and the pressures and requirements of daily life. The new worldview gives rise to a sense of optimism and a spirit of generosity. The higher self appears. The features of traditional spirituality at its best are automatically fostered.

It all spells an extraordinary freedom. The great mystery glimpsed in childhood reawakens because absolutely any physical possibility is a real possibility in the unlimited future. We are the pilots of our holographic universes, blazing along through time in parallel. Now it is time to come into our own and participate fully. As Meijer closes his article on Wheeler, ending with his wonderful optimistic insight:

> To know that all of us have a role to play in the universe, should matter to each and every one of us and motivate us to take our personal responsibility. When we become real participants, we may truly make our world, and the universe as a whole, a better place for ourselves and all that is living. Ultimately we may even understand our own position in this grand design, as Wheeler formulated splendidly:
>
> "*Someday we'll understand the whole thing as one single marvelous vision that will seem so overwhelmingly simple and beautiful that we may say to each other: 'Oh, how could we have been so stupid for so long? How could it have been otherwise!*" Wheeler (2002). (2015, 20)

The new physics tells us that there is vastly more to us than we imagined. We are the fields of information that define our holographic universes, at cause and immortal. It is the best conceivable kind of existence once we understand it. This is the new intelligence.

The New Intelligence

At present most of us are primarily identified with the ego, and we generally operate on just the low moral rules, the set of principles laid down by law and social convention. It seems ordinary, but egoism is the cancer that slowly immolates the soul, and is now destroying the functional integrity of the human culture. It is born of a sense of isolation because it is identification with only a part of the psyche, the ego, and the rest is alien. It is quite literally smallness of mind. It is a disaster for the individual because it inevitably leads to hellish futures. It is a collective catastrophe because rampant combative self-interest automatically leads toward all kinds of Armageddon.

It is the high moral rules of altruism that form a key component of a fully successful society. This is the basis of a high level of group identity and cooperation. This is what makes communities work effectively. Evolved over millennia, this instinct is what gave our human race the unique level of coordination to develop civilisation, and the power to take over the planet. But with the atomisation of the culture in the Internet age we are seeing the consequences of the breakdown of this vital component of society enacted, a vast tide of egoism and separatism, and thus the ever-increasing likelihood of self-annihilation. The collective human culture is exhibiting the hallmark symptom of severe clinical depression – contemplating suicide.

As Jung describes in *Modern Man In Search of a Soul* (1933, 229), once the numinous has gone from life one will not be healed until it is found once more. In other words, a sense of higher purpose beyond simple ego gratification is a fundamental requirement for a healthy psyche. This is entirely natural in the light of our evolutionary history. As Darwin explains, we are inherently empathic beings, highly social animals that naturally feel a need for connection to the greater whole.

The new worldview heals because it reconnects us to nature, religion in the literal sense. It is clear that one is deeply involved with every aspect of the known world, at cause and immortal. By comparison, living solely as the ego is desolation. With this understanding the enormity of the future of one's life returns to us the awe and wonder so lost. The meaning of life is that all possibilities are truly open.

The Participatory Age

With this new worldview people more naturally adopt the high moral rules. Consequently a new intelligence emerges, and a new efficiency permeates the human culture. This is the next step. The new worldview means interactive destiny but also responsibility, immortality but also karma. At some deep level of the psyche it seems we have always known this. The greatest myths are poetic depictions of real principles in the operational reality. Far from an irrelevant speck in the destiny of your world, you are the director. A daunting level of responsibility but with prizes unimaginable.

Great sages of antiquity have provided us with the instruction manual for this kind of existence, the Buddhist Noble Eightfold Path. This is the Reality Health & Safety Manual for the personal world. The Ten Commandments provide the quick-start guide. Living in this way you interact with the destiny of your holographic universe in ways that produce only good karma. Only positive strange attractors are generated. This is not only building a better life here and now but also defining the best possible architecture for the next. So enlightened egoism is the only sane life position. Thus the implications of the new physics form a scientific rationale for the methodology of true success as described in long-standing wisdom.

Nothing is impossible, and to add to the whole is to flourish. In a culture of this nature the high moral rules become the default position, as they are in all good families. As a result all kinds of new opportunities become real, possibilities currently unimaginable. This is the ideal society of order and inner peace endlessly imagined, a fabulous, mythical, supposedly lost age. But the higher-self culture is a perfectly feasible future. It is a natural consequence of understanding who we really are and how reality actually works.

By picturing the ideal world, not only for oneself but for everyone, and making it as real as possible in every way, we move toward it in reality. And by communicating the rationale we evolve the effect. The scientific revolution of the new physics culminates in a new transformative worldview. A new age of humanity is born.

PART 2

THE SCIENCE

"The state of physics today is like it was when we were mystified by radioactivity. They were missing something absolutely fundamental. We are missing perhaps something as profound as they were back then."

David Gross (2005)

17

The Triune Ontology

Physics is the science of what everything is made of and how it all works. Perfectly naturally, a single overall 'ontology', the basis of all existence, is assumed – physical reality. But key features of reality are totally incompatible with this worldview: the passage of time, the Now and wavefunction collapse, aka the 'measurement problem'. The resolution is that these paradoxical phenomena are operating at different 'levels of logical type'. Rather than a single ontology, there are three fundamental categories of existence. This is the basis of the new worldview presented here that resolves these hitherto intractable paradoxes.

Logical Type

The principle of logical type was discovered by the polymath Bertrand Russell (1908). It is quite simple, but the implications are profound. A class of things is a completely different type of thing to a single element of the class, as a population is to a person. The class inevitably has quite different kinds of properties. This is why the superworld is a holographic universe while the objective reality is a quasi-classical world. As he shows, failure to make this distinction inevitably leads to nonsense results and paradox. As shown here, the paradoxical phenomena are operating at different levels of logical type to the quasi-classical world assumed. This is the deep thing that the new physics is trying to tell us about how the world works. In the light of this triune ontology the new physics makes perfect sense.

The Second Logical Type

The great paradox in quantum theory is the collapse of the wave function. This is the change of the quantum state, the fundamental definition of physical reality, from indeterminate to determinate, whenever it is observed. The problem is that this change is brought about by passive observation. It seems that just looking at something has an effect on the physical reality. Which is nuts, a classic nonsense result. The quantum state is the basis of all existence. Passive observation cannot make any difference to it. The resolution is that no such thing happens. There is no change in the objective physical reality itself. Only the superworld of the inside view changes.

So how does that work? How does the quantum state of that physical reality change? Logical type is the key to the solution. You cannot change the colour of a glass marble, but you can easily change the colour of a jarful of marbles, by changing the class of marbles in the jar. This is a second-logical-type phenomenon. Individual marbles stay the same, but the result is different. The superworld is of the same logical type as the jarful of marbles. It is an entire class of worlds superposed to form a world: a 'class-of-worlds-as-a-world'. Collapse is change of the definition of the *class*. This resolves the great paradox.

For this kind of physical reality it is perfectly natural that the quantum state changes when an observation is made. Observation only changes the definition of the world hologram, but *that* changes the definition of the class of worlds in which it exists. Like the different jarful of marbles, the new definition defines a different condition.

The quantum state of the superworld is defined by the superposed sum of all the worlds in the class. So when the class changes, the quantum state changes. Collapse operates. The missing key is that this is a second-logical-type operation. The physical world itself does not change, just as the glass of each marble stays the same colour. The paradox is the result of the assumption of a single quasi-classical world, a category error of logical type. This is completely invisible in the modern paradigm of physicalism, hence a century of frustration.

The Third Logical Type

The great paradoxes in relativity are the passage of time and the Now. As described in Part 1, modern physics shows us that there can be no such phenomena. Time is a dimension, a static continuum in the four-dimensional space-time of the universe. As Weyl describes, quoted in Chapter 9, the moving viewpoint of consciousness is the solution. And of course we all have direct evidence of this phenomenon. The Now is constantly experienced passing into the future.

By definition, this moving viewpoint cannot be a part of physical reality. That is all static and fixed. It has to be to the worldline as the projector is to a movie film. The frames in sequence on the film define the first-logical-type, 'primitive', elements of the system. The film as a whole is a second, 'higher' logical type of entity. It has the resulting property that it can be played, brought to life. The projector mechanism is completely different kind of thing again, a third logical type: it operates on any and all films. It is to the movies as a movie is to the single frames. It has the property of bringing to life.

Just as the projector makes frame after frame along the celluloid film to be the current image, consciousness makes moment after moment along the worldline to be the Now. It is necessarily a third-logical-type phenomenon. As described in detail in the next two chapters, this accounts for how reality actually works.

Three Phenomena

So the new worldview demonstrates a threefold ontology, at the three different levels of logical type. Physical reality is ontologically fundamental, 'ontic', as we naturally assume. This defines the first-logical-type attributes of the physical entity, each physical object, system or entire world. These are defined by the quantum state in the conventional manner. The superworld is a different type of physical entity, a whole class of worlds, a second-logical-type phenomenon. As this superposition of worlds defines the quantum state, this is ontic also, on the inside view. Universe consciousness is the third-logical-type phenomenon. It is inherently ontic. As Weyl states, quoted in Chapter 10, this consciousness does not belong to the world. The experiencing consciousness has to be a property of the universe itself. Because this is rigorously excluded from the science of physics, the essential 'motor' of physical reality is missing, and the paradox of the Now is insoluble.

The key phenomena at the three levels of logical type are quintessentially different. We know them all well, but their essential natures have not been fully recognised. The *matter and energy* of the system define the first-logical-type domain, the ordinary world; but this is a static definition, exactly like each frame of a movie. A *field of information*, the world hologram, defines the second-logical-type domain, the superworld actually encountered, as described in Part 1. The world hologram itself is ontic because it defines the class of worlds forming the superworld. That is why the superworld changes as each observation changes the world hologram. The result is the ongoing appearance of a physical reality changing, the holographic-universe movie of life. *Consciousness* is the iterator of the system, bringing the movie to life, a totally different kind of thing again. This is the 'projector'.

It is this triune ontology that finally makes sense of the new physics. The paradoxical phenomena are not bizarre and inexplicable properties of the quasi-classical world but processes at different levels of logical type. The collapse of the wave function on observation is a second-logical-type phenomenon in the superworld. The holographic universe updates. The passage of time and the Now are third-logical-type phenomena, properties of the universe as a whole. Part 2 lays out the explanation of the physics at the root of all this. The next three chapters address the paradoxes of relativity in a bit more depth, and the wonder of genesis, and then we dive into quantum theory.

18

The Passage of Time

Relativity means that physical reality is a static, four-dimensional 'block universe'. To explain the passage of time a moving viewpoint is a fundamental requirement, but this cannot exist in physical reality.

The Block Universe

For most of human existence, the nature of time has been a great mystery. Saint Augustine describes what we all tend to feel:

> What then is time? If no one asks me, I know: if I wish to explain it to one that asketh, I know not. (Chadwick, 2008, 230)

With the advent of relativity this problem was solved. Time is a straightforward linear dimension. It is essentially just the same kind of thing as each of the three dimensions of space, except that it is invisible to us.[2] This is not in question, but the inevitable implication is very strange. The entire four-dimensional extent of space-time just exists. Nothing moves, and nothing changes. As Deutsch states:

> Spacetime is sometimes referred to as the 'block universe' because within it the whole of physical reality – past present and future – is laid out once and for all, frozen in a single four-dimensional block. (1997, 268)

---

2 Mathematically it differs from the dimensions of space in having the imaginary number *i* as a component: the square root of minus one.

As he goes on to explain in some detail, this means there cannot be any such thing as the passage of time. The whole universe is static, and the entire span of physical reality, throughout time, is all 'there'.[3] This is the direct implication of the basic math of Einstein's relativity, which is both simple and endlessly proven correct. The evidence is clear and irrefutable. As demonstrated by leading physicists, the proof is the 'Andromeda paradox' briefly described in the Glossary.

Given the static block universe, only one kind of solution is possible, a moving viewpoint. This is an absolute requirement. There has to be something that is to physical reality as the projector is to the frames of the movie film. And since nothing physical can be in this position, Weyl's explanation is the only one tenable. The gaze of consciousness moves along the worldline, through the space-time of the block universe, into the future. This is what gives rise to the experience of the passage of time.

As you drive down a dark road in the night, your headlights make a flood of light that moves along the road with you, lighting up one section of the road after another, always lighting up the road where you are. In a logically identical way the viewpoint of consciousness moves along the time dimension 'lighting up' each moment in turn. All the moments are already there in space-time, just as all of the road exists in front of you, out of sight. All that happens is that the gaze of consciousness passes along through space-time into the future. As a result, moment after moment is experienced in sequence. This is what is experienced as the passage of time.

---

3 Note that in cosmology the term 'static universe' means something quite different. In cosmology, it means a universe that is not expanding. But the science shows that our universe *is* expanding, getting bigger *as time passes*. But time does not pass: the universe is static in *that* sense, as Deutsch explains. This means that at future times, the universe is bigger than it is today, but the whole four-dimensional totality, including all the future sizes it will be, exists 'already', static, permanent.

Physicalism

Weyl was a highly influential mathematician, theoretical physicist and philosopher, and a close friend of Einstein's, but his solution is not taken seriously because there is no possible way this movement can be a physical phenomenon. His explanation is simple and elegant but it is automatically rejected because it is directly at odds with the current paradigm. In the current scientific worldview of modern physics, physicalism is taken for granted. The solid belief that nothing exists independently of the physical world, in any way, is generally adopted. According to the basic tenets of today's scientific worldview, there *can* be nothing other than the reality of matter and energy.

So although the nature of consciousness is unknown, it is taken for granted that it must, obviously, be just a property of the physical brain. Like everything else, therefore, it would be stuck in time, a static part of the static physical layout of the universe. So it cannot possibly move through time. As Deutsch emphasises:

> It is often said that ... our consciousness is sweeping forwards through the moments. But our consciousness does not, and could not, do that. ... *Nothing* can move from one moment to another. To exist at all at a particular moment means to exist there for ever. (1997, 263)

This is perfectly true of the psychological consciousness, that which gets experienced. As described in Chapter 10, this is just a property of the brain, and so cannot possibly move through time. At each point in time there is a specific state of the psychological consciousness, fixed, static, a property of that particular moment, at that point in space-time. But the experiencing itself, the universe consciousness, is of an utterly different nature. This is what cannot make sense in the physicalist worldview of modern physics. But as directly demonstrated by the experience of the passage of time, that is simply wrong. As described in the next chapter, leading physicists have held the view that consciousness passes through the static universe.

Since the moving viewpoint cannot be a physical phenomenon, this is taken to mean that it simply does not exist. So in this case the general assumption is that the passage of time must be some kind of illusion. But it is of course as real as can be, as we all experience. There is no question that I am getting older. In this case Weyl's simple but radical explanation is the only possible solution. The passage of time is the effect of the moving viewpoint of consciousness, passing through space-time, up the worldline. As described in the next chapter, this is the natural explanation of the Now, the ever-moving present moment that constantly passes into the future along the life-line of the body. As a result there is the experience of moment after moment. In effect, time passes.

19

The Moving Now

The consciousness explanation of the passage of time is vehemently denied whenever it is raised. It seems that this solution is literally unthinkable in the context of modern physics. So in that paradigm, if the passage of time cannot be a physical phenomenon it cannot be a real phenomenon, so it must be some kind of illusion:

> ... it appears that the flow of time is subjective, not objective. ... I and others argue that it is some sort of illusion. (Davies, 2006a)

> ... time is not an illusion, but the flow of time is. So is change. (Tegmark, 2014, 176)

In one sense this is true, since time itself does not actually flow, and things do not actually change, but this is not just a trick of the mind. It is the universe in operation. This is confirmed by the solution to an even bigger problem, the Now. That is the real showstopper.

The Now

Physicist David Mermin explains the issue very clearly in his article in *Nature*:

> My Now — my current state of affairs — is a special event for me while it is happening. I can tell my Now from earlier events, which I only remember, and from later events which I can only anticipate or imagine. The status of an event as my Now is transitory: it becomes a memory as subsequent Nows emerge.

> Yet clear, evident and banal as this is to us all, there is no Now in the usual physical description of space and time. Physicists represent all the events experienced by a single person as a line in four-dimensional space-time, called that person's 'world-line'. There is nothing about any point on my world-line that singles it out as my Now. (2014)

The paradox of the Now is a hugely significant problem. As the philosopher Rudolf Carnap records, Einstein once told him that the problem of the Now worried him seriously:

> He explained that the experience of the Now means something special for man, something essentially different from the past and the future, but that this important difference does not and cannot occur within physics. (1963)

That something so central to reality *cannot* exist in the physics means that relativity is an incomplete description of the world. No wonder Einstein was disappointed. But it *is* a full and complete description of the *physical* world. The Now is something completely different.

Each event in my life exists at a particular point in space-time, a point along my worldline, a specific moment, like each of the moments depicted in Figure 9. Objectively, none of these moments has any special status. They all just exist, laid out in space-time. But as the moving viewpoint arrives at each moment, it becomes the Now.

The Now is simply the moment being experienced, in the moving viewpoint, as it passes along the worldline. One moment after another becomes the Now, acquiring this special status, as the moving viewpoint arrives at that moment. This is how the Now, the present moment, moves from moment to moment along the worldline. Mermin's description of the Now is quite literally the description of the effect of the moving viewpoint of consciousness.

Given that there can be no such phenomenon in physical reality, Weyl must be right. Consciousness does not belong to the world. The Now is a third-logical-type phenomenon.

The Movie of Life

The Now that cannot be explained in the physics, the moving viewpoint of consciousness, is what brings the real world to life, iterating the moments along the worldline. As stated by philosopher of science Michael Lockwood, quoting the eminent physicists Arthur Eddington and Sir James Jeans:

> ... events do not happen; they are just there and we come across them ... In this case our consciousness is like that of a fly caught in a dusting-mop which is being drawn over the surface of the picture; the whole picture is there, but the fly can only experience the one instant of time with which it is in immediate contact. (2005, 54)

Just as the viewpoint of the fly moves across the canvas of the picture, the viewpoint of consciousness moves up the worldline of the body, along the sequence of moments in time. Clearly, Lockwood, Eddington and Jeans accept the obvious implication. Consciousness passes through time, bringing the static world to life. This is the only logical explanation. This is how reality actually works. This is what gives rise to 'transtemporal' reality as described in Chapter 28.

As Tegmark states, space-time is just like a movie. The whole worldline of your life exists laid out 'already'. At each moment, sitting there in the future, there is a specific state of your world hologram, including your perceptions of that moment:

> All your subjective perceptions exist in spacetime, just as every scene of a movie exists on its DVD. (2014, 268)

In other words, the you of yesterday, and even the you of tomorrow, are every bit as real as you right now. This is all part of your worldline, like all the frames of a movie on a DVD. As Tegmark goes on to say, the movie of life does not run. The universe is static. The resolution is that the moving Now produces the *effect* of the passage of time, and the *appearance* of reality changing – the movie of life, Weyl's fleeting image in space which continuously changes in time.

Retrodicted

The moving Now cannot make sense in the current paradigm. In apparently unrelated news the nature of the experiencing consciousness is a total mystery also. Both paradoxes remain insoluble. The solution to both these longstanding puzzles is that the experiencing consciousness is universe consciousness. And the Now is the moving viewpoint of this consciousness. This is the answer to the great question posed by Hawking: "What is it that breathes fire into the equations?" (1988, 174). It is universe consciousness. This is just how reality actually works.

Despite the superb fit with the facts, the idea of consciousness being anything other than mundane is usually rejected automatically. This has even been labelled 'quantum mysticism' as described in Appendix VI. Weyl's concept is just too alien to modern physics so it is ignored, and the quest to find an explanation in physical science continues unabated. Nonetheless, this is what we have actually discovered. We have just been unable to take it in. Given this understanding, the apparently insoluble paradoxes of the Now and the passage of time are automatically resolved. Indeed, these phenomena are 'retrodicted', meaning this is the explanation of scientific facts we know for sure but have not been able to understand. These seemingly paradoxical phenomena are third-logical-type attributes of the universe.

20

Genesis

The world hologram is a field of information. It is produced by the brain. It is experienced by the universe consciousness. It is the identification of the consciousness with the world hologram that gives rise to the 'transtemporal' individual, meaning an entity who is existing through time. This kind of being has free will.

Identification

As described in previous chapters, given that we are experiencing the passage of time in the static block universe, Weyl must be correct. And this means that the experiencing consciousness is necessarily a property of the universe as a whole. But since it is omnipresent, it must be experiencing all of the perceptual realities of every possible person in the universe, all possible world holograms, all at once. But all that is ever experienced is one specific particular perceptual reality, 'this one', *my* reality. The reason is that, in each case, consciousness can but identify completely with *this* perceptual reality. As Bitbol states, referring to consciousness as the ubiquitous Mind:

> Indeed, as soon as (abstract) Mind identifies itself with a point of view, it can but identify itself to a *particular* one. ... the point of view Mind adopts, when adopted, is not one among others; it is *the* point of view, self-referred to as *my* point of view. (1990, 8)

The reason is that the world hologram defines everything determinate in this reality, and so there is nothing else to know. Consciousness can but identify completely with this particular field of information because in this frame of reference this is all the information there is in the whole world.

The way light works is a useful metaphor for this identification. Suppose I am looking at a picture in the sunlight. The picture that reaches my eyes is all light, but it is no longer full spectrum white light. It has taken up the pattern of information defined by the picture. That is all the information there is. Similarly, the universe consciousness takes up the pattern of information defined by the world hologram, and that is all the information there is.

Each conscious individual is a dynamic entity created by the experience of the world hologram by the consciousness. The universe consciousness is the experiencing *I*, 'in here', at the centre of the world hologram, utterly familiar yet so incomprehensible. The *me* is the world hologram, the individual in reality. The identification of the consciousness with the world hologram is the genesis of the conscious individual, the *me* experienced by the *I*.

It is because consciousness is universe consciousness that we come to be transtemporal beings, experiencing moving through time in an ever-evolving reality. The result is the experience of a new version of the world hologram in moment after moment, the experience of life in action. This is how the movie of life runs.

Free Will

This identification also explains why there is free will. Intuitively it seems obvious that one has free will, but in the real world everything is predetermined. As described in Chapter 4, Newtonian mechanics defines a world as predictable as clockwork. Certainly, the quantum world is defined in terms of a branching tree of possibilities rather than the single track of classical physics, but that does not mean free will. The layout of the tracks, each one a specific sequence of events, branches into all possible tracks, but each track is a fixed and static part of the structure. No being *in* one of these tracks, no individual in physical reality, can possibly have free will.

Consciousness, on the other hand, is in precisely the correct logical position to make executive choice. Its essential nature is contextual to physical reality. Like Tegmark's bird in Chapter 7 it is effectively outside of the world. Thus it is in the correct logical position to be able to switch the viewpoint one way or the other. Clearly, nothing else is in this position. But the problem with this is that the consciousness has, by itself, no criteria. It has no point of view about what would be good, or right, or desirable, any more than the movie projector has a favourite movie, or wants the plot to go a certain way. As Bitbol describes:

> Mind is by itself point-of-view-less, just as it is placeless and timeless. (1990, 8)

It is infinite and unbounded, so it encompasses everything, and thus all possible points of view. The net result is that it has no particular point of view. Thus it has the capability to make choices, but no criteria. As described in Appendix VII, it is not in any way a person.

But exactly the opposite is the case when it is identified with the world hologram of a particular individual. This identification gives rise to an emergent entity, the conscious individual, the *me* experienced by the *I*. And this entity, of course, does have a set of criteria, often of immediate importance. And decisions are taken. And which version of the future is likely to be experienced is altered. This is free will. Conscious individuals make real choices.

To put it more formally, free will is a property of the emergent entity that arises from the identification of universe consciousness with the world hologram. The first is free, having the capability of choice. The second has will, volition. Thus conscious individuals have free will. And this means that we can operate interactive destiny deliberately. This is how the game of life actually works. The full nature of the transtemporal conscious individual is described in Chapters 29 and 30.

And There Was Light

There is a remarkable implication that arises from the nature of the conscious individual. We all begin in unison. The first experience of the life-line of any organism with visual perception is the awareness of light. At this point absolutely everything else is indeterminate. Only subsequently to this beginning does the world hologram develop, recording experiences and thus defining the character of this entity, and the nature of the environment, along with all the other facts of life.

This is the inside-view big bang. At the very beginning of every life, every *me* is identically the same, just the experience of light. So to universe consciousness there is only one of this beginning. This is the first experience of all world holograms that go on to become sapients. So on the inside view all such life begins in unison. And as life goes on, with each observation made the original lifeline endlessly branches.

There could be no witness to the real big bang, but the spiritual myth of genesis applies perfectly to the initial moment of conscious individuals in unison. In the very beginning there was light, out of the dark of non-being. As stated by the philosopher Gilbert Ryle:

> A myth is, of course, not a fairy story. It is the presentation of facts belonging to one category in the idioms appropriate to another. To explode a myth is accordingly not to deny the facts but to re-allocate them. (1949, 8)

The myth of genesis is exploded to reveal a powerful integrative force in our philosophy. The birth of the psyche is a unitary experience, literally common to us all. We were all one in a universal origin.

21

Quantum Reality

While relativity has long been fully accepted, the paradoxes of quantum theory are seen as so severe that its validity is questioned, despite its 100% empirical success. This chapter describes the fundamental principles in the physics of the quantum world, and the apparent paradox that has plagued quantum theory for a hundred years. Experiments show that observation, just looking at something, makes the physical world determinate. Following chapters explain the resolution, based on logical type as described in Chapter 17. This is illustrated by Schrödinger's cat and Wigner's friend in Chapters 25 and 27.

The Quantum

The quantum is the fundamental building block of physical reality, the basis of all physical existence. Everything is made of quanta. The quantum is a very peculiar thing, which is what makes quantum theory so famously weird. Whenever physicists perform an experiment to measure the exact location of a quantum, such as an electron, it is found to be a tiny particle in a specific location, just as one would expect. But unobserved, a quantum is nonetheless not in a specific position. It exists in a different form, as a spread-out wave, as illustrated in Figure 21.1 below. And the wave defining a single quantum may be spread over inches, miles or even light-years. This is what human science has discovered. No question this is the fundamental definition of physical reality, very strange though it seems.

The Wave Function

The mathematical definition of the quantum is the wave function. Just like a physical wave on water, the wave is bigger in some places and smaller in others, usually in a characteristic pattern. But this is not a wave of something physical, like water in a pond, or the air pressure that we experience as sound. It is a wave of probability. The bigger the wave, the greater the probability of the quantum particle being found to be there, if an observation is made with a detector. This probability wave is mathematically defined by the Schrödinger wave equation, discovered in 1925. Schrödinger received the Nobel Prize in 1933. This is the foundation of quantum mechanics, the operational mechanics of the quantum.

Figure 21.1 illustrates the wave function of a single quantum that is passing through two very narrow slits in the grey wall at the top of the image. The quantum could be a quantum of energy, such as a photon of light, or even a quantum of matter, such as an electron. The wave function defines every possible position where the quantum could be found to be, if an observation is made.

That is all there is. That is the fundamental definition of existence. Strangely, therefore, as has often been noted, the fundamental stuff of reality is really non-stuff. So said Werner Heisenberg, who won the Nobel Prize in 1932 for the creation of quantum mechanics. He stated clearly that the elementary particles, the quanta, are not real things in the same way as the phenomena of everyday life:

> ... they form a world of potentialities or possibilities rather than one of things or facts. (1962, 128)

Figure 21.1 The wave function of a single quantum passing through two slits.

This aspect of quantum theory is no longer theoretical. We know for sure that reality is indeed of this nature. It has been tested to greater degrees of accuracy than any other theory in scientific history with 100% success. Experiments such as this well-known 'double-slit experiment' are conclusive. Waves of probability of this nature are the fundamental basis of all physical existence.

The Superposition Principle

This explains the phenomenon of 'quantum superposition'. This is a fundamental principle of quantum mechanics. It means that two quantum systems can be simply added together, just like ordinary waves. Waves on water in Figure 21.2 demonstrate that effect. The ring patterns originating at the two gaps in the wall add together to form an interference pattern shaped very like the quantum wave in Figure 21.1. This explains why even whole worlds can simply add together. The fundamental definition of any physical system is a mathematical waveform, the wave function, thus even entire worlds add together just like the waves on water.

Collapse

Not just energy, but even the solid matter of reality behaves as a spread-out wave of this kind, except when observed. But then, the moment it is observed, the quantum is found to be a specific actuality, a 'point particle': a tiny particle of matter at a specific position. This is the famous collapse of the wave function that gives rise to all the trouble in trying to understand quantum theory.

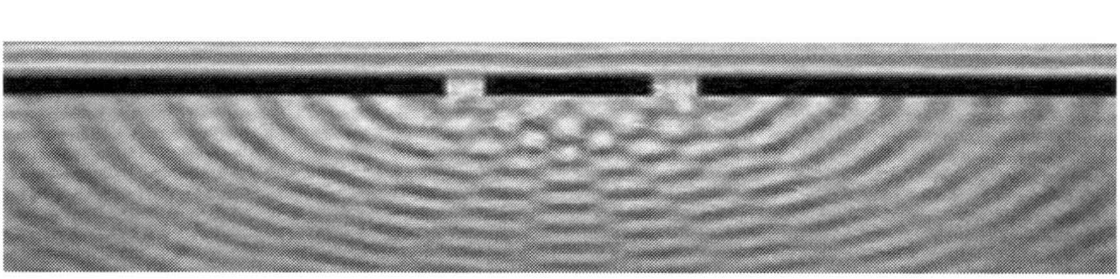

Figure 21.2 Waves on water passing through two openings in a wall.

As numerous variations on the double-slit experiment make clear in practice, the collapse dynamics is a real phenomenon. But the question of how this happens, why this happens, and even whether or not it does in fact happen has been the subject of heated debate ever since the discovery of quantum theory a hundred years ago. This is the measurement problem, described in following chapters. As with the problem of the passage of time, very few of us have even heard of this problem but it has occupied some of the greatest minds.[4]

At first, the discovery of the collapse of the wave function was taken at face value, as a physical phenomenon. This formed the basis of the Copenhagen interpretation developed by the famous physicist Niels Bohr and his colleagues. He received the Nobel Prize in 1922. This theory holds that unobserved, physical reality is nothing but waves of probability; but whenever the state of the physical system is measured, just making an observation, the wave of probabilities collapses to a specific state of being. Thus reality is determinate, meaning it is defined as specific physical entities in specific states, when, and only when, someone looks at it. It is a far cry indeed from the ordinary Newtonian classical world. As Bohr tartly commented:

> Anyone who is not shocked by quantum theory has not understood it. (Gribbin, 1984, 5)

Despite seeming crazy, this became the standard view of quantum theory, still favoured by many physicists. But it makes no sense. Observation is a purely passive action. Nonetheless, the evidence is irrefutable. Without question, observation gives rise to determinacy. This is what the double-slit experiment reveals. The quantum always appears as a specific tiny dot somewhere on the detector screen.

---

4 Note that the idea has been repeatedly put forward that the interference phenomenon of 'quantum decoherence', described in Appendix IX, is a full and sufficient explanation of the appearance of collapse. However, as stated by numerous experts, this is not the case. The 'preferred basis' problem means that the operational frame of reference of this phenomenon cannot be defined. The solution is described in Appendix X.

22

Many Worlds

The whole fundamental issue remained in limbo for decades. Eventually, in 1957, Hugh Everett came up with the perfect solution to the measurement problem. There *is* no collapse. But there is the *appearance* of collapse. This is the basis of his famous many-worlds theory.

In this case, if there is no collapse, then all possible versions of events get played out. And this means that all possible versions of the world come into being. This is where the many-worlds concept originally came from in physics. Figure 22.1 illustrates this idea with Alice being asked out by Bob. Naturally, she may say yes or no.

If there is no collapse, then both possibilities happen. Effectively therefore, the world splits in two, and both versions exist. In one version of the world she said yes, and in another version no.

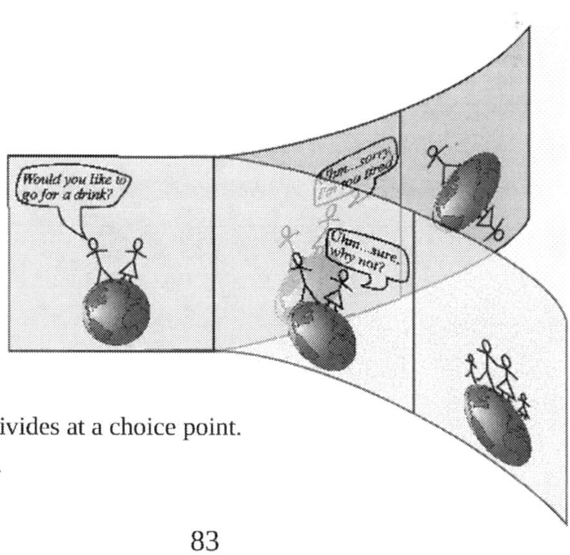

Figure 22.1 Reality divides at a choice point.
Gratis Max Tegmark.

The World Splits

The weirdness of this splitting, and the crazy super-abundance of all possible worlds, were far too strange to be even considered at the time. The whole thing was automatically rejected. Everett was first studiously ignored and then ridiculed. The worldview of the time held that the universe was very clearly a single physical world, end of story. But he saw that this was a false assumption, directly at odds with the physics. He simply took the physics, the wave function, at face value; and this means that all possible worlds exist. Finally, half a century later, it is increasingly accepted that he was obviously right.

However, the full meaning of his concept is still the source of intense discussion and wildly differing views. This is not surprising because what he actually states is that a specific unique reality exists *only* in experience. Since this cannot possibly make sense in the current physicalist paradigm, there has been an endless quest to find a way of making his explanation work in terms of physical reality. Half a century of intense and expert focus has produced no solution. This is described in detail by the philosopher Jeffrey Barrett in his book *The Quantum Mechanics of Minds and Worlds* (1999). Everett's theory resolves the paradoxes, but makes no sense in physical reality.

Making Observations

Here is how it actually works in us humans. Everett's concept centres on the technical process of making an observation. The human body uses the sensory apparatus, the eyes, ears and so on, to detect the sights and sounds of the world. And the neural system of the brain turns all this information into a visual image, with a sound track. Right now you are experiencing a visual image, a view of reality, specifically some words in black on a white background. That is simply the information, in the form of an image, that you are actually experiencing 'in here'. This is the visual representation 'in here' of the reality 'out there' that the brain produces.

That representation *is* the observation. It is the recording of this image in memory that is the making of the observation in physics.

This process, over time, produces the vital, central component of his formulation – the state of the memory, defined as the record of the observations. The state of the memory is the sum total of all the sensory information that gets experienced and recorded in memory. The integrated synthesis of this record of observations forms the world hologram. In other words, the world hologram is the state of the memory, the key component of Everett's formulation.

Now for the bit that gives rise to all the difficulty. This is what he actually says in his conclusion. When the observer interacts with the environment, and an observation is made, the result:

> ... is a superposition of states, each element of which assigns a different state to the memory of the observer. (1957, 462)

The superposition of states means that the physical reality *itself*, including the observer, becomes literally the superposed sum of both situations at once. This is depicted in Figure 22.2. But, in each state, on the inside view, there is a different, specific state of the memory. As he goes on to say: "Judged by the state of the memory", i.e. on the inside view of each of these physically superposed states, there is just one specific version of the event observed, as shown in each branch of Figure 22.1.

In other words, physical reality works like Figure 22.2, but the experience of the world hologram works like Figure 22.1.

Figure 22.2 In physical reality both versions of reality exist superposed.

Experience

Everett is saying that on the outside view both versions of reality are real and present, coexistent, simultaneously. In other words, physical reality itself is a superposed mishmash. But on the inside view there is a single, specific outcome to the observation. So objectively both outcomes are real, but in experience, and only in experience, there is just one single outcome to events. Thus there is the *appearance* of collapse as he emphasises. In other words, there is collapse, but only on the inside view, only subjectively, in experience.

In the current physicalist worldview this makes no sense, so it is generally assumed this is not what he really meant. But this is exactly what he really meant. This is the central point of his theory. In his conclusion he clearly states: "It is found that experiences of the observer" (1957, 455) are in full accord with the predictions of the standard formulation of quantum mechanics, based on collapse.

The big question is how does this work? What does the state of the memory have to do with the determinacy of physical reality? As Barrett describes in exhaustive detail, there is no way to make sense of this with regard to the physical world, as defined by all of physics to date. Everett is essentially saying that the physical realities of the outside view and the inside view are different, but there is no explanation of how this could be so. You saw it here first! As has been described, the reality encountered on the inside view is a completely different type of domain, a superworld. And in this type of physical reality the determinacy is defined solely by the observations experienced. So collapse happens automatically on observation because this changes the definition of the physical reality on the inside view.

The paradox of the collapse dynamics arises because of the assumption of a quasi-classical world. This is of course a perfectly reasonable assumption, but it is this fundamental category error that has given rise to all the difficulty in comprehending the quantum theory. We are actually doing all our experiments on a superworld.

23

The Invisible World

The superworld is the missing ontology of Everett's formulation, but this different type of world is deeply obscure because although it is in fact a radically different kind of world, it looks exactly like an ordinary world. It is only what is unseen that is indeterminate.

Ordinary Appearance

The record of observations is identical in all the superposed worlds, so by definition they all look identically the same. So the superworld, all of them superposed, looks exactly like an ordinary world.

And it behaves exactly like an ordinary world as well; but only as long as we don't do any quantum physics experiments. When we do classical Newtonian physics experiments, dropping balls off the leaning tower of Pisa, we always get a straightforward, classical result, even though we are in fact experimenting on a huge number of worlds all at once. This is because all the worlds give identically the same result, so the superposed sum gives that result. So it even seems to operate just like an ordinary world. It is only when we do quantum physics experiments that we see that the underlying physical reality is a superposition of worlds. This is the meaning of Schrödinger's cat as described in Chapter 25. It is a perfect illustration that the physical reality on which we are experimenting is a superworld. This is what the physics of Everett's formulation describes, the operation of a class-of-worlds-as-a-world.

Different Types of World

As Tegmark describes, referring to Everett's many-worlds universe as the multiverse, this defines two very different types of world:

> From the bird perspective, Everett's multiverse is simple. There is only one wavefunction, and it evolves smoothly and deterministically over time without any kind of splitting or parallelism. The abstract quantum world described by this evolving wavefunction contains within it a vast number of classical parallel storylines ("worlds"). (Tegmark, 2007, 3)

Both types of world are well known in modern physics. As physicist Brian Cox states of the objective world of the bird perspective:

> There is only one 'world', and it is a world in which everything that can happen does happen and everything is in a superposition with everything else. (2017)

Nonetheless, effectively, there *are* real discrete quasi-classical worlds, as stated by philosopher of physics David Wallace:

> "Worlds" are mutually dynamically isolated structures instantiated within the quantum state, which are structurally and dynamically "quasiclassical". (2011, 17)

These worlds are all in the same place at the same time, all superposed as Cox states. This is the original understanding of Everett's theory by physicists Wheeler and Graham, as quoted on page 91.

What has been totally invisible is that neither type of world is the one that Everett is addressing, defined by the record of observations. He calls this the 'relative state'. Logical type makes it all clear. The "worlds" in the multiverse are quasi-classical, first-logical-type domains. The world of the observer is of this nature. But the world that operates as Everett describes is the world of the individual on the inside view, the second-logical-type superworld. The one 'world' Cox describes is third logical type. Without the explanatory principle of logical types, the different nature of the relative state has been invisible.

24

The Holographic Universe

As a description of the solid quasi-classical world, the holographic universe makes no sense. As physicist Jacob Bekenstein describes:

> The holographic principle states ... that volume itself is illusory and the universe is really a hologram which is isomorphic to the information "inscribed" on the surface of its boundary. (2003, 59)

So the holographic universe is usually depicted as a weird sphere at the outer edge of the objective physical reality of the cosmos, which is clearly ludicrous, a nonsense result. But the holographic universe is just the cosmological form of the superworld, and it is perfect sense. Physical reality is all described on the screen of the observed surface.

Superworld Cosmology

As Smolin describes, quoted in the Preface, there is no question that the holographic universe is a real phenomenon of some kind. It means that the three-dimensional world is completely defined on the two-dimensional boundary at the outer edge.[5] This is precisely the nature of the superworld, Everett's relative state. The world hologram both forms the outer boundary of the physical reality encountered, and defines the determinacy. This therefore produces the *effect* of the holographic universe. But the world is nonetheless entirely real.

---

5 The evidence is definition of the 'entropy' of the system, a fundamental property of physical reality, as described in the Conclusion.

The three-dimensional world is not an illusion. Every world in the superposition that forms the superworld is a real solid three-dimensional world. So the holographic universe is all perfectly real because it is 'made of' solid three-dimensional worlds. The holographic universe is just the *effect* of the superposition. The net result of the superposition of worlds is a physical reality defined solely by the world hologram, which forms the outer boundary. So the real holographic universe is defined at the outer boundary of perception, not the outer limits of the physical cosmos.

The superworld, the second-logical-type domain of the class-of-worlds-as-a-world, defines the ontology of Everett's relative state, and also that of QBism. It is determinate solely where observed. The resulting cosmology, the physical form of the superworld, is the holographic universe. This is the evidence for the nature of Everett's relative state, a completely different kind of world to the quasi-classical world. So the exact form of the real world directly encountered has long been discovered and examined in depth, but without a trace of recognition. Again, we *have* discovered what the world is like, but it has been just too weird to be taken seriously.

This also confirms the principle of multi-solipsism, the network of interacting, personal, physical, parallel realities. As Smolin concludes:

> The world must be a network of holograms ... the holographic principle is the ultimate realization of the notion that the world is a network of relationships. Those relationships are revealed by this new principle to involve nothing but information. (2000, 178)

Our communications, speech, writing and so on, form the information that passes from one individual's reality, one holographic universe, to another. Just as Mermin describes of the personal realities of QBism:

> When I converse with you ... we can arrive at a common understanding of our external worlds, in spite of the privacy of our individual experiences. (2014)

25

Schrödinger's Cat

Schrödinger's cat is a famous thought experiment. There is a fifty-fifty chance that a cat in a box has been killed by a quantum device. According to standard quantum mechanics the cat is then in a superposed state of dead and alive at the same time, as in Figure 25.1.

When someone looks inside the box, the cat is of course either alive or dead; but that action is an observation, which makes it determinate. Unobserved, it must be dead *and* alive. Obviously, that makes no sense. Schrödinger deliberately posed the idea in this way to illustrate the absurdity of the quantum theory, but actually it is fully correct.

The resolution is that the cat is indeed both alive and dead, but in different versions of the world. As stated by Bryce DeWitt, the first prominent physicist to take Everett's many-worlds theory seriously:

> Schrödinger felt that the wave mechanics that led to this paradox presented an unacceptable description of reality. However, Everett, Wheeler and Graham's interpretation of quantum mechanics pictures the cats as inhabiting two simultaneous, noninteracting, but equally real worlds. (1970, 31)

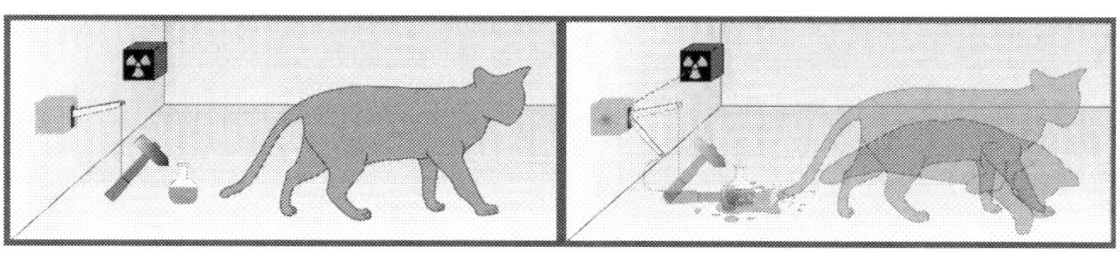

Figure 25.1 Schrödinger's cat.

Objectively, both versions of events do happen. Thus both physical realities exist, as in Figure 25.2. So in the grand scheme of things there is no question that the cat is both alive and dead at the same time – in parallel realities, each one a specific quasi-classical world. The key point is that the experimenter is in both worlds.

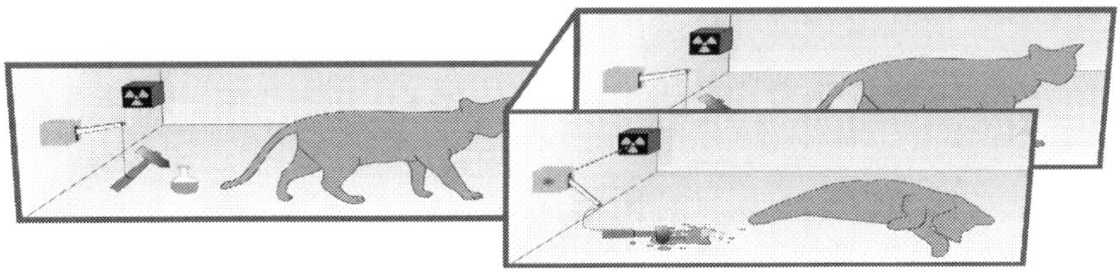

Figure 25.2 Parallel worlds of Schrödinger's cat.

Category Error

The explanation of Schrödinger's cat is quite straightforward in the context of a superworld. For Schrödinger, before he looks inside the box, his superworld contains both versions of the world. So for him the cat really is both dead and alive because his class of superposed worlds includes both of the different versions of the world. Naturally, therefore, for him, the state of the cat is the superposition of both, as in Figure 25.1. This is described in detail in the next chapter.

The paradox of Schrödinger's cat arises because the wrong type of frame of reference is taken for granted. It is a category error of logical type. Which is easily made when the world in which experiments are carried out looks exactly like an ordinary world. But it is a superworld, a second-logical-type phenomenon with very different properties. This is the meaning of Schrödinger's cat. In the context of an ordinary quasi-classical world the result is absurd, a nonsense result as Schrödinger so creatively illustrated. But this is just how a superworld works. Dead and alive *can* only be a second-logical-type phenomenon.

26

Collapse

The collapse of the wave function is simply explained. The moment Schrödinger observes inside the box, this observation defines him as existing only in one specific version of the world or the other. This logical dynamics is graphically illustrated in Figure 26 (Lockwood, 1989, 231; adapted). The cylinder represents all the possible versions of Schrödinger's worldline in his superworld. Each one exists in a specific quasi-classical world. The worldlines in which the cat dies are on the left, and those in which it survives on the right.

In the lower section, before the observation is made, Schrödinger sees only the outside of the box, so at this point his world hologram is the same on both sides. Thus his class-of-worlds-as-a-world contains both versions of physical reality, dead cat and alive cat. So in the physical reality of his superworld, his holographic universe, the cat really is alive and dead at the same time.

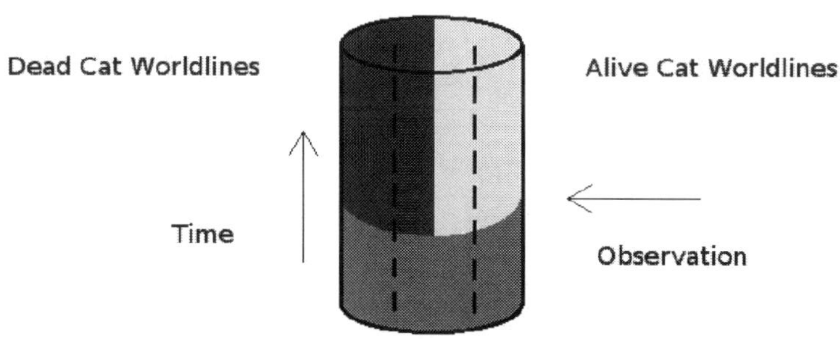

Figure 26 Parallel worlds in the Schrödinger's cat experiment.

Then, once the observation is made, his superworld includes only the worlds in which, say, the cat is alive, the sunny yellow version. His superworld is all that changes, but for him the effect is collapse. Meanwhile, of course, the version of him that observed the cat dead also exists, in a different parallel superworld, the sad blue one.

The Appearance of Collapse

This explains Everett's appearance of collapse from first principles. When an observation is made, and the definition of the world hologram changes, the definition of the class-of-worlds-as-a-world changes – it becomes the class of only those worlds in which *this* observation was just made. This is the enactment of the collapse dynamics. Nothing physical changes. As Everett states, in emphasis throughout:

> ... *it is not so much the system which is affected by an observation as the observer, who becomes correlated to the system.* (1973, 116)

Correlations are described in Appendix X. Each observation generates a correlation between observer and observed. Schrödinger becomes correlated with either one version of the world or the other.

Passive observation of thc physical world does not, of course, change the physical world one jot. But there the appearance of collapse, in the physical world, for the individual making the observation, just as Everett describes. The reason is that the making of the observation alters the world hologram, and this alters the definition of the class-of-worlds-as-a-world. This is how the reality encountered actually changes. This is described in detail in Chapter 28.

Naturally, the paradoxical weirdness applies only to Schrödinger on the outside of the box, in his superworld. For the cat in his superworld the outcome is never in question. All his worlds are the same, all death or all life. Schrödinger and the cat are not in the same superworld, and thus have different physical realities. Cats have always known this.

27

Wigner's Friend

The Wigner's friend paradox is essentially the same thought experiment, but including a second observer in the experiment itself. It was presented by Eugene Wigner, a theoretical physicist and mathematician who won the Nobel Prize in 1963. Wigner's friend makes an observation. For instance, this is Schrödinger, observing the state of the cat. Quantum theory tells us that for Wigner, who is elsewhere, the whole situation is not just unknown but indeterminate: as with Figure 22.1, not only which version of the outcome happened but also what the consequences were, and so on is all indeterminate.

Personal Parallel Realities

The explanation of the paradox is the same as in Schrödinger's cat, For Wigner, his friend is in different, determinate states, in different versions of the world, like the cat in Figure 25.2. So for him the state of his friend is indeterminate. The meaning is straightforward but highly significant. The direct implication is that different individuals live in different, personal, physical, parallel realities. As held in QBism, quoted in Chapter 3, what is real for an agent rests entirely on what that agent experiences, and different agents have different experiences. As this means that for us the universe is a multi-solipsism.

Wigner's friend has now been confirmed in experimental physics. This means that physical reality is 'observer-dependent', i.e. idiosyncratic to the observer. As physicist Alexander Poltorak describes:

> … Massimiliano Proietti at Heriot-Watt University in Edinburgh and his colleagues performed an experiment designed by Brukner and tested Wigner's Friend Paradox by entangling six photons. They proved that two contradictory realities could coexist. Eugene Wigner was right; the quantum reality is observer-dependent. (2019)

This is meaning of the fundamental tenet of Everett's theory, quoted in Appendix X. Physical reality is relative to the individual, thus different for different people.

Interactive Destiny

We have no choice about being swept along together through the time of space-time, but we are constantly steering our personal paths through the infinite possibilities of the quantum universe. Interactive destiny means that we are the directors of our personal, physical, parallel realities, our holographic universes.

Our realities run in parallel because for the most part our holographic universes are identical with regard to all the big stuff, the layout of the world, the way things work and so on: the stuff that 'everyone knows'. So we are all sweeping along through space-time together, in parallel realities which are generally much the same. It is with respect to our lives in the world of human affairs that individuals' holographic universes may differ wildly. Our superworlds define different destinies. As the physical reality is idiosyncratic, relative to the individual, so is the future. This is a big help in making sense of interactive destiny. It is of course a purely personal phenomenon.

Of course, even as a personal phenomenon it still sounds like a denial of everything sensible we know from modern physics, but logically it is inevitable. The full technical explanation is found in the 'quantum concept of time' as described in the next chapter.

28

Two Types of Time

With the advent of quantum theory we have discovered that there are two different kinds of time in operation. We are used to the idea of progressing through time, from the past into the future. That is the time of classical physics. Relativity shows us this is simply one dimension of the four-dimensional space-time. But there is another, completely different kind of time also in operation, as Deutsch explains in Chapter 11 of *The Fabric of Reality* (1997). Quantum time is the time evolution of the quantum state defining the physical reality. It seems obvious that this is just what happens as we progress through space-time, but this is a completely different type of process, operating in a different type of dimension, 'Hilbert space'. This is a 'state space', meaning that every point within it defines a specific state of the system. We experience the passage of time in relativistic time, but we encounter change in quantum time. Interactive destiny operates in quantum time.

Snapshots

The dynamics of the wave function is called the linear dynamics. This is the dynamics of the fundamental components of the physical reality of the world, the quanta. With the time evolution of this dynamics, the state and arrangement of all the matter and energy in the world changes and progresses in a linear, predictable manner.

This is all defined by a specific quantum state. The key point is that this defines not only state of the world at the present moment, but also throughout all of the past and all of the future. This therefore defines a physical 'snapshot' of the whole world, as Deutsch calls it, the whole physical reality of the world, defined by a specific quantum state. As he explains, the quantum universe is the totality of all possible snapshots, and this is the basis of the quantum concept of time. Change of the quantum state is the transition from one snapshot to another. Here the snapshot is the holographic universe of the individual.

Figure 28.1. symbolises one snapshot. This illustrates the worldline of an observer, the trajectory through the four-dimensional spacetime of the world, going up the page into the future. Each of the flat planes symbolises one moment in time. The linear dynamics of the wave function defines the whole of this worldline, for all time.

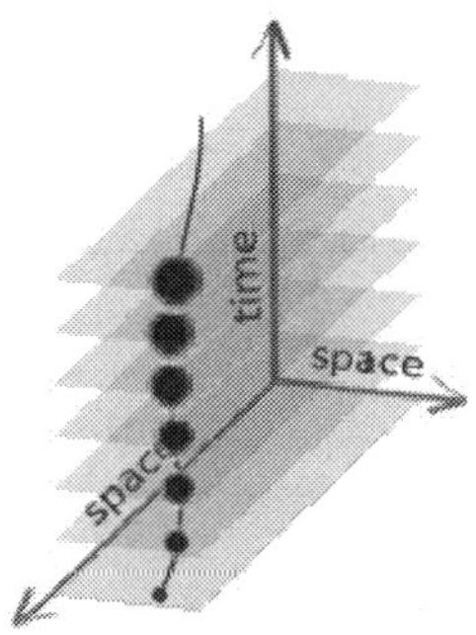

Figure 28.1 The Worldline.

The further we look into the future, the more the wave function spreads out like ripples on a pond, as shown back in Figure 21.1. This means that what will be observed at a given moment in the future is increasingly indeterminate. This is symbolised with the blobs becoming more and more vague going into the future. This figure symbolises a process that is all contained within a specific snapshot, i.e. the world defined by a specific quantum state, defining a specific wavefunction.

The progression of the linear dynamics is shown by each white arrow in Figure 28.2. This is what is experienced as the passage of time. Then, at the point in time where an observation is made, something completely different happens. The superworld changes, thus a different quantum state defines the physical reality. The collapse dynamics operates. There is a different snapshot. This is shown by the black arrows. The small dot symbolises the effective collapse to determinacy of the blob. This is experienced as the observed event happening.

This process happens in Hilbert space, a different kind of dimension to the dimensions of relativity. As Lockwood states, this is:

> ... a new dimension running, so to speak, perpendicular to time and space. (1989, 232)

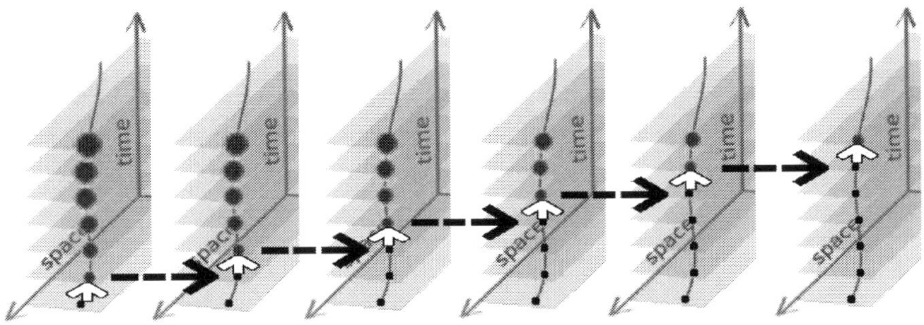

Figure 28.2 A sequence of snapshots in the quantum concept of time.

In the next snapshot the progression of the linear dynamics operates, and thus there is the alternating operation of the two dynamics. These are the different types of time of the two pillars of the new physics. In relativity, other times are just other points along the time dimension of space-time, as is obvious. In the quantum concept of time, other times are other snapshots, whole space-time definitions. As Deutsch states:

> This is the distinctive core of the quantum concept of time:
> Other times are just special cases of other universes. (1997, 278)

The Moving Viewpoint

Both types of time, however, are static. Relativity and quantum theory agree completely. As Deutsch states, quantum time does not happen either. As stated by physicist Julian Barbour, a specialist in time:

> The quantum universe just is. It is static. (1999, 256)

The only thing that can possibly happen in the static physical system is that the viewpoint moves, as Weyl describes. This is what gives rise to transtemporal reality, passage through time. The root cause of this phenomenon is described in Appendix XI. This explains how both dynamics do effectively operate in the unchanging block universe.

Within the context of a snapshot, the viewpoint of consciousness passes along the worldline into the future. Thus the linear dynamics is effectively enacted, and there is the appearance of the passage of time as Weyl describes. Then, when an observation is made, the viewpoint moves 'sideways', to a different snapshot in Hilbert space. Thus there is the appearance of the change of the quantum state in objective physical reality, just as Everett describes. In experience the dynamics cycle, as described in the textbook formulation quoted in Appendix XII. The two types of time alternate.

Interactive Destiny

Once we comprehend the quantum concept of time, interactive destiny makes perfect sense. This explains the actual mechanics. On the inside view each snapshot is a holographic universe, defined by a specific quantum state. When an observation is modified before it is added to the record of observations, the moving viewpoint arrives in a different snapshot, a different version of the holographic universe, on the path taken though the infinite possibilities. The diagram only shows one black arrow in each case, but in reality there are many possibilities, leading to different places in Hilbert space, different versions of the holographic universe with different futures. It is not, of course, that we can change or in any way influence the physical reality itself. The facts of the future are totally set and fixed in the permanent destiny of each snapshot. But as each observation is made, one passes to a different snapshot. As we can deliberately bias this process we can effectively pilot our way in the constantly branching stream of the multiple-choice movie of life.

29

The Protagonist

In this chapter and the next we explore the nature of the conscious individual in the new paradigm. In this chapter the central significance of the individual in the physics is addressed. In the next the full definition of the individual is described, including the structure of the psyche. The term protagonist refers to the entity for which both dynamics, linear and collapse, are real operational phenomena.

The "Observer"

As we have seen, the only protagonist of the collapse dynamics is the world hologram, the mind, but this is completely absent from modern physics. As Nobel Laureate Frank Wilczek writes:

> The leading interpretations of quantum theory introduce concepts that are extrinsic to its equations ("observers"), or even contradict them ("collapse of the wave function"). The relevant literature [on the meaning of quantum theory] is famously contentious and obscure. I believe it will remain so until someone constructs, within the formalism of quantum mechanics, an "observer", that is, a model entity whose states correspond to a recognizable caricature of conscious awareness, and demonstrates that the perceived interaction of this entity with the physical world, following the equations of quantum theory, accords with our experience. That is a formidable project, extending well beyond what is conventionally considered physics.

> Like most working physicists, I assume, perhaps naively, that this project can be accomplished, and that the equations will survive its completion unscathed. In any case, only after its completion might one legitimately claim that quantum theory is defined by the equations of quantum theory. (2006, 142)

As he indicates with the scare quotes, the missing protagonist, the "observer", is not the observer in the sense usually assumed, the physical entity. The entity he describes is the world hologram.

Firstly, the world hologram is not just a caricature of conscious awareness but its full and precise definition. This *is* the conscious awareness, the perceptual reality. This is the key component of Everett's formulation, central to the physics. The "observer" is a field of information. Secondly, there is no question that the perceived interactions of this entity with the environment follow the equations of quantum theory exactly. That is the whole point of Everett's thesis:

> It is found that experiences of the observer ... are in full accord with predictions ... of quantum mechanics (1957, 455)

It is the entity formed by the experiences of the observer, the world hologram, that is the "observer" that is missing from the physics. In other words, there is a precisely world-hologram-shape hole in the science. As we have seen, it is the superworld of this "observer" that operates the paradoxical collapse dynamics, and thus resolves the measurement problem, and explains Schrödinger's cat.

The Hidden Protagonist

What makes the nature of the "observer" highly obscure is that there are actually two different protagonists in the physics. The observer, meaning the physical body, is the protagonist of the physical dynamics, the linear dynamics of the wave function. Nothing happens to the world hologram between observations. So, with respect to the unfolding development of physical reality in the passage of time, the physical observer is indeed the protagonist, as is quite naturally assumed in the science of physics. But with respect to the collapse dynamics, the progressive change of the quantum state in physical reality, the only protagonist is the world hologram. The physical body remains in a superposed state. This is what Everett is actually saying, as described in Chapter 22. But this explanation requires accepting the central importance of experience in the physics, and this is rigorously excluded in the physicalism of modern views.

Wilczek describes the crucial missing component of the quantum theory, the conscious entity that encounters the collapse dynamics. All the while, exactly this protagonist is the central component of Everett's formulation, though he does not mark it out clearly. It is only in the many-minds explanations of his theory that a protagonist other than the physical observer is explicitly defined. And only in Lockwood's *'Many Minds' Interpretations of Quantum Mechanics* (1996) is the protagonist specifically defined as the sum of experience, the 'phenomenal perspective'. This, finally, is what resolves the great problems with quantum mechanics, as he demonstrates. His theory is described in Appendix XIII. The superworld is the ontology of his theory. The holographic universe is the reality.

The key point is that the world hologram, and only the world hologram, encounters both dynamics. The world hologram *follows* the linear dynamics, along with the observer, as it only can. Then, when an observation is made, the superworld of the world hologram *operates* the collapse dynamics. Thus only the world hologram follows both dynamics, and encounters both types of time in action.[6]

6 As described in Appendix XIV, the perceiving subject is the vital missing component essential to making sense of the physics because it actually embodies the logical types missing from the science. The second-logical-type world hologram explains the dynamics of collapse in the world. The third-logical-type consciousness that experiences the world hologram explains how the dynamics come to actually operate.

30

Identity

The world hologram is the functional identity, meaning this is the whole of what makes you who you are. This is the field of information that if uploaded into a new body, as in *Altered Carbon*, would mean that the whole of the real you was now living in this new body. It includes not only all the memory of one's life, but also the particular way one makes decisions and lives one's life, all the functional traits, the way one operates. This is the real you 'in here'.

As described in Chapter 8, the self-avatar figure is the integrated synthesis of all the observations of the self. The classification of the self-avatar figure as distinct from the rest of the world hologram is inherent in the structure of Everett's formulation. He defines the observer as a machine, a device that records: "... sensory data and machine configurations" (1957, 457). The integrated synthesis of the observations of sensory data from the world at large gives rise to the world hologram. The observations of machine configuration are the observations of oneself, and the integrated synthesis gives rise to the self-avatar figure at the centre. All together this is who you really are.

The Real Person

As described in Chapter 8, even the body is indeterminate except where observed. This is an inevitable property of a reality defined solely by observations. As von Baeyer states, explaining QBism:

> If I am the agent, the objective world is everything outside my mind—including other agents and even my own body. All of that I may, if I chose, treat quantum mechanically and describe by wavefunctions. (2016, 154)

He is defining the mind as "… my own experiences and perceptions" i.e. the world hologram. This sounds so surreal, but the logic is the same as for the rest of the objective world. In the class of worlds superposed to form the superworld, every possible body that instantiates this world hologram is included. Thus only what is observed is determinate because only this is the same in all these worlds.

This is only on the inside view of course. On the outside view the DNA defines all your physical characteristics in detail. This is the blueprint of the body, and the reference data by which all new forms are generated in the physical system. But in your superworld, every possible variation of the DNA that produces a body with your world hologram is included in the class-of-worlds-as-a-world. Thus all the things the DNA defines about you are indeterminate, except for those things that are observed, or learned about through medical technology.

The Mind

With respect to the body this indeterminacy is a strange idea but no big deal. All the basic components of your body are nonetheless quite well defined. You cannot see inside your body, but proprioception means that you experience the position and mass of bones and muscles as it operates, fairly precisely. It is only the details that are indeterminate. But with respect to the mind the result is fascinating.

The word mind is generally taken to mean the activity of the neural network of the body as a whole, including all its operational attributes. But on the inside view only the memory, meaning the world hologram, is determinate. The word mind is here used to refer solely to the world hologram. This is the same definition as in Lockwood's formulation, the sum of all the experiences.

In this context the rest of the system is 'outside' the mind, along with the body. All that is here taken to be the operating system of the body, like a computer operating system that comes with the computer. It is an attribute of the observer machine. The body comes with an operating system, and you, the world hologram, live 'inside' it. As von Baeyer states, that is all part of the world outside of the mind. The operating system hosts the mind, but on the inside view the two are operationally distinct. The mind is the real person 'in here'.

This leads the extraordinary implication. Just as your world is a class-of-worlds-as-a-world, your brain is a class-of-brains-as-a-brain. And this means that in effect your brain works like a quantum computer. It carries out all possible variations of your internal processes simultaneously. This would appear to be the explanation of the ineffable magic of creativity as described in Appendix XV.

The Unconscious

The new paradigm explains the functional difference between the three major attributes of the psyche that Jung (1969) describes, the conscious mind, the 'personal unconscious' and the 'collective unconscious'. The conscious mind is the immediate awareness of experience, the 'contents of consciousness', meaning the view of reality that is currently being perceived. This is the sensorium, as symbolised in Figure 6.1. This is the observation currently being added to the world hologram. The rest of the world hologram is the personal unconscious, the record of past observations. As Jung describes, this is all the aspects of the memory, laid down by experience, that could be accessed consciously but are not in conscious awareness at the moment. This is the unconscious mentioned in Chapter 15.

He also defines the collective unconscious, something quite different. As he describes, this psychic component is not formed in the mind of the individual but is a feature of the inherited structure of the brain. It contains certain pre-existent forms, the 'psychological archetypes'. These are generic outlines or models of specific types of person. Each has a typical personality, a pattern of behaviours that make up a certain way of being, and they can play a major role in influencing how we think and feel and act. This is all part of the generic operating system of the body, developed over evolutionary periods of time. It is collective because this is shared among all humans.

The Functional Identity

The world hologram is the me 'in here', the record of observations forming the personal unconscious plus current observation being made. This is the functional identity, the protagonist in reality. This too follows from the physics. As Everett states:

> ... the actions of the machine at a given instant can be regarded as a function of the memory contents only, and all relevant experience of the machine is contained in the memory (1957, 457)

As Deutsch states, quoted in Chapter 12, everything about the way one operates in the world is expressed in the virtual reality of the world hologram. In other words, the world hologram is your functional identity, meaning this is who you really are as an operational entity, a living person. The machine in which this individual lives is the body with its operating system. The collective unconscious is an attribute of the operating system and thus all part of the machine.[7]

Taken all together, this is the standard objective identity, the body with the mind 'inside' it. This is the identity I am used to of course. It seems obvious that the whole thing is what I really am. But on the in-

---

7 Because it is outside of the mind, this explains the remarkable kinds of properties Jung described. He observed that these archetypes can be energised in the service of mass politics. Powerful symbols such as patriotism and rights can be used to energise the collective unconscious to produce powerful emotional responses to a simple message. So just as computers can be hijacked when the operating system is hacked, we can be manipulated en mass outside our conscious awareness.

side view the world hologram is what I really am. The body is just the physical vehicle in which I reside. I am the world hologram, the functional identity, the mind experienced by consciousness, the transtemporal protagonist. I have a body.

The Triune Identity

There are three different types of identity, at the three different levels of logical type: body, mind and spirit. Notably, this trinity of different fundamental natures is recognised in the Gnostic trinity of early Christianity, as described in Appendix VII. This trinity of natures is the reason that the full nature of personal identity has been so impossible to understand properly. The physical body with its complex operating system is the ordinary identity. But on the inside view it is indeterminate except where defined by the world hologram. The world hologram, the mind, is the only determinate entity. The spirit is the universe consciousness that experiences the mind and breathes life into reality, the *I* that experiences this *me*. All together this forms the standard identity of the conscious individual, a human being with all its extraordinary properties.

We are triune, existing at three different levels of logical type. We are of course physical beings, but we are primarily beings of information, world holograms in action. You are a holographic movie of life, experienced by consciousness. However strange this might seem it means you really are immortal. The one thing certain about your next lifetime is that your record of observations will be intact. Effectively, in the continuity of experience, as the world hologram, you are reincarnated. So when the consciousness passes on from one lifetime to the next it is the whole of the real you, your entire mind, that wakes up in the next lifetime. It is the real you, the functional identity, with all your memories and your self-concept, in a new body.

31

Conclusion to Part 2

There is a triune ontology, three fundamental operational categories of existence. This is what makes the new physics make sense. The mysterious and seemingly impossible attributes of reality are not just explained but retrodicted, meaning this explains scientific facts we know for sure but have not been able to understand. This is the evidence. These are phenomena at three different levels of logical type.

We know from direct experience that the movie of life is running, although the universe is static. When consciousness is understood as a third-logical-type phenomenon this makes perfect sense. This is how reality actually works. We also know from direct experience that just one specific version of events happens at each moment although the universe gives rise to every possible version. This collapse is an inherent feature in the physical reality of the individual on the inside view. This is the time evolution of a superworld, a second-logical-type phenomenon. This explains how reality actually changes. A new version of the holographic universe becomes the reality with each observation made.

Unexpectedly, the implications of this new worldview reveal an urgent and crucially important opportunity. This counteracts the egoism wrecking the global human culture and flirting with Armageddon. Perhaps the deepest challenge to acceptance is the nature of our true selves. We are the world holograms that define our holographic universes, experienced by the consciousness.

Quantum Theory

The paradoxes of the quantum theory have remained unresolved for so long, despite being examined by so many first-rate minds, that it has been mooted that the solution is beyond our grasp. But the objective was always to explain the paradoxical collapse dynamics in terms of the quasi-classical world of the linear dynamics. The unwelcome discovery is that a physicalist solution of this kind cannot be found. The explanation is that the paradoxical collapse dynamics operates only in the superworld of the inside view, a second-logical-type domain. It is like trying to understand the dynamics of a whole class of people by intensely studying a single individual. The two incompatible dynamics are the time evolutions of these two different domains in their different cosmologies. Schrödinger's cat, dead and alive, can only be a second-logical-type phenomenon. This is what has been discovered but not recognised. In retrospect it is obvious.

The evidence is the holographic universe, the cosmology of the superworld. This is a real phenomenon as shown by the 'entropy'. This fundamental feature of physical reality is defined solely by the surface of the domain. As Bekenstein (2003, 59) explains, the entropy of ordinary mass is proportional to surface area and not volume. This means that without question the quantum universe is a surface phenomenon, a holographic universe. The superworld is the ontology.

Relativity

The peculiar paradoxes of relativity are generally of little interest because the theory itself is taken as gospel. If human experience seems not to conform to the equations, then no doubt sometime in the future we will come to understand why. And the answer will be something to do with human experience, *not* relativity physics. All true. There is nothing wrong with the actual physics. The phenomena that the physics cannot explain, the passage of time and the Now, are third-logical-type phenomena.

The subjective effects of the present moment, and time passing, cannot be deduced from the formal structure of physical reality, the four-dimensional, space-time, block universe. That is like trying to work out what makes trains work from the layout of the track. The third-logical-type consciousness is required.

The missing explanatory principle is the moving viewpoint of consciousness, as Weyl describes. This explanation works perfectly, but sadly this has been even more unacceptable than incomplete science. In the current paradigm there is no room for such a concept. As Deutsch emphasises, *nothing* can pass through space-time, and he specifically includes consciousness. But as Weyl states, the experiencing consciousness does not belong to the world. Deutsch and Weyl are both right, at different levels of logical type. Nothing can move from one moment to another at the first, primitive level of logical type. Everything in reality is part of a specific moment, just as Deutsch states. But the consciousness Weyl refers to is of an utterly different nature. It is universe consciousness, a third-logical-type phenomenon. This is how reality actually works.

Who You Really Are

The missing piece of the puzzle is the nature of the conscious individual. You are body, mind and spirit. These are the three types of identity at the three different levels of logical type. Modern physics arrives where all science began and the place is fully known at last.

We generally grow up versed in the idea that we are ordinary physical entities, and that the world is quite separate from oneself. On the outside view this is as true as it is obvious. As a body one is simply an observer, a physical machine with sensory apparatus and memory, as Everett describes. And apart from minor phenomena the body is indeed utterly separate from the rest of the world. But on the inside view the truth is very different. You are the world hologram, and you define the holographic universe you know as the world.

Hence Macrocosm Microcosm. In effect you are the world you know as physical reality.

In operational terms you are deeply connected with all of it, and the same is true for each one of us. This is a multisolipsism. It means you are the unconscious director of the whole of your reality, the pilot of the path taken by your holographic universe through the infinite possibilities of the quantum multiverse.

We are empowered and we are responsible, but we have been pilots asleep at the wheel. Denying any plausibility to myth and spirituality the baby is gone with the bathwater. As irrelevant specks it is every speck for himself. But this is a dangerous delusion because karma operates. Quite unaware, we have been constantly generating strange attractors, and thus interacting with our destinies, often in ways which are not helpful, even disastrous. Awareness transforms the situation. We can take charge, pilot deliberately, interact with destiny on purpose. Following the guidance of the great spiritual rules, things get better. Egoism evolves into enlightened self-interest, and the higher self appears. This heals people individually, and also fosters the survival and prosperity of the race.

We are nodes in a multi-solipsism in the space of all possible worlds. I am the director of my holographic universe. It is a massive and terrifying discovery. I am responsible for a domain greater by far than I had conceivably imagined. I feel a bit like Slartibartfast, Douglas Adams' world-weary architect of worlds as he alerts the earthling Arthur Dent (ellipses in original denote pauses):

> I should warn you that the chamber we are about to pass into does not literally exist within our planet. It is a little too . . . large. We are about to pass through a gateway into a vast tract of hyperspace. It may disturb you. . . . It scares the willies out of me. (1979, 97)

The new paradigm defines a daunting new cosmology. Your personal holographic universe is a world-size solipsism, and *everything* is defined by the world hologram, your mind. And immediately beyond the limits of that boundary lies the indeterminate totality of all possible worlds, quite literally a vast infinite hyperspace.

As this is who you really are, what you observe is of central and critical significance, hence the reality of karma and the unreasonable effectiveness of creative visualisations. This is the *INTERACTIVE DESTINY* upgrade for global empowerment and responsibility. As the experiencing consciousness is universe consciousness you are effectively immortal. This is the *PHILOSOPHER'S STONE* upgrade. Dare to know!

APPENDICES

"As human beings, our greatness lies not so much in being able to remake the world – that is the myth of the atomic age – as in being able to remake ourselves."

Mahatma Gandhi

1

Paradigm Shift

Thomas Kuhn was a highly influential philosopher of science whose research transformed the way science is understood. The publication of his book *The Structure of Scientific Revolutions* (1962) became a landmark event in how science itself is understood to work. His key concept is that major scientific discoveries about how the world works always entail great upheavals, 'scientific revolutions', meaning changes which are hugely resisted. Major discoveries in the new physics such as Max Planck's discovery of the quantum, and Hugh Everett's explanation of its dynamics are vivid examples. Superb breakthroughs are not only disavowed but reviled.

The Worldview

We all form a concept of the world, a mental model of reality that enables us to find our way about and interact with it. This is primarily a map of the world in the literal sense, defining where places are and how things are arranged. This is how you remember where you put your keys down. But it also includes an understanding of how things work, and what things are likely to happen. All this as a whole is one's worldview. When it changes, the effect can be shattering.

We now know that the Earth is not flat, and it is not the centre of the solar system let alone the universe of galaxies. Now we know that the worldview of those who went before us was quite wrong. Now we know the truth, the old worldview seems simplistic and quaint, and the new worldview is obviously correct. But when Copernicus first put forward the idea of the Earth going around the Sun in 1543 it was unthinkable. It seemed it could not possibly be right. Eventually there was a massive revision of the current worldview, a scientific revolution, and as a result a different worldview held sway.

Out of Sight

Mostly, we are all naturally resistant to changing our worldview, but Kuhn realised that there was more than this at work. As he explains, once a worldview has become a 'paradigm', by which he means a deeply-held and well-structured concept of the world, a new concept that is incompatible with it is *automatically* rejected. It seems clear it is just obviously wrong. Thus if new research indicates there is a fault in this worldview, this is not seen as refuting the current paradigm but just a mistake by the researcher, however prestigious. This shows that the rejection of new ideas is not a deliberate or even a conscious process. But as he describes, this leads to a classic Catch-22:

> Once it has achieved the status of a paradigm, a scientific theory is declared invalid only if an alternate candidate is available to take its place. (1962, 77)

The physicist Hermann Weyl noted this exact response to the new physics, saying that physicists and philosophers both continued to:

> . . . stick stubbornly to the principles of a mechanistic interpretation of the world after physics had, in its actual structure, already outgrown the latter. They have the same excuse as the land person who for the first time travels on the open sea: he will desperately try to stay in sight of the vanishing coast line, as long as there is no other coast in sight, towards which he steers. (Scholz, 2004, 3)

There has been no new coast in sight. So since the requirement of a viable alternative has not been met, the current worldview has remained stuck while the science carries on without an explanation.

The next great scientific revolution has stalled. Meanwhile, theories such as QBism are not taken seriously just because they are far too strange, far too remote from the coast line of the current paradigm.

Stuck in this cautious atmosphere for a hundred years, it has come to seem that there is no hope of any explanations for the weird paradoxes of the new physics, so generations of physicists have learned to just ignore the weirdness. "Shut up and calculate!" as physicist David Mermin (1989) famously joked. But the problem is so acute that the meaning of the physics even became an embarrassment, actually taboo. As cosmologist Max Tegmark states:

> To tell the truth, I think most of my colleagues are terrified of talking to philosophers -- like being caught coming out of a pornographic cinema. (Musser, 2002)

Clearly something with deep psychological roots is going on. This is explained by the work of neurobiologist Mark Changizi, as described in Appendix II. The principles behind the phenomena Kuhn addresses are very clearly defined in his work on domains of expertise.

The New Lexicon

It is not just reactionary unease that stands in the way of new understandings. As Kuhn explained in his later work, another problem is that deeply novel ideas usually require a new 'lexicon', meaning the vocabulary of new terms that define the key features of the new explanation, and without which it does not make sense. The lexicon that has been missing in the new physics is 'logical type'. This is described in Part 2. It is the lack of this further dimension of explanation that produces the great paradoxes. As described in the text, there is nothing whatsoever wrong with quantum theory or relativity. In both cases the paradoxes arise because the phenomena that are inexplicable in the context of the current paradigm are operating in a completely different way to what is naturally assumed.

II

The Field of Exploration

As Kuhn explains, the existing worldview has tremendous stasis. Neurobiologist Mark Changizi has identified a phenomenon which makes the power of the existing worldview so absolute that this becomes inevitable. In the light of his explanation one can see why the problem is so ubiquitous that Kuhn reports it as a principle.

As Changizi explains, on joining a community of scientists one's abilities become sharply honed to focus on differentiations within the field of interest of that community. This, however, tends to go hand in hand with a loss of the ability to see a broader view.

Adaptation

He describes the process by likening it to going from brilliant daylight into the poorly lit space of a room underground. At first one can see barely anything because everything looks dark, and it is more or less impossible to discriminate between one shade of dark and another. But one's vision quickly adapts, and then one becomes able to see clearly, making the usual fine discriminations of vision within this darker context. This process is called adaptation. As he describes, it also operates in the intellect. Joining a community of experts as a non-expert, the fine discriminations being made in the community are almost impossible to pick out. But one gradually adapts, becoming an expert in the field. The problem is that as part of this process the horizons tend to shrink to that of the domain under attention:

> When we enter a creative community, varieties of adaptation mechanisms are automatically elicited inside us, helping to illuminate the intellectual world inside the community. Ideas within the community that were impossible for us to distinguish become stark oppositions. ... In order to make it happen, though, you underwent a kind of "world shrinkage" ... our full range of reasoning is brought to bear on a narrow spectrum of ideas, a spectrum that we're under the illusion is as wide as it can be. And so we don't realize the world has shrunk at all. (2009)

Our horizons shrink but we have no idea. So something obviously wrong, which could be seen in a different light, is just dismissed.

Here we have a highly plausible description of the origins of the stasis of scientific experts, harshly lampooned by Max Planck:

> A new scientific truth does not triumph by convincing its opponents and making them see the light, but rather because its opponents eventually die, and a new generation grows up that is familiar with it. (1949)

This is now known as Planck's principle. He discovered the quantum, and outlined quantum theory, and he became deeply frustrated and increasingly infuriated by the endless non-acceptance of his results.

Shape Up or Ship Out

Just the shrinking of the horizons of the domain cannot, however, be the whole story. This does not explain why the outer boundaries of the domain under study are not tentatively explored, and seem to become *completely* invisible. As Changizi explains, this is due to a profound but unconscious commitment to the paradigm:

> We're social primates, and a full human life is centered on the communities we're in, and our place within them. There aren't many hermits, and most that are probably wish they weren't. Communities of people have bulls-eyes on them that are irresistible to us humans. (2009)

In other words, we need to belong. And as he describes, the requirement is that people in the group are like-minded. So in order to belong we have to join in the worldview of our group wholeheartedly.

This is the emotional fuel that powers the integrity of the worldview of a community. This explains the origin of Kuhn's central points. Firstly, one does not want to be different. Secondly, the whole group, or in some cases a whole culture, would have to change.

Newbies

Finally, as Changizi notes, the brightest individuals are strongly attracted to the communities within which the paradigm is most precisely defined. As he states of the most creative communities:

> Not only are these creative communities dangerous to one's creativity, but they seductively attract creativity-seeking individuals into them like moths to a creativity-scorching flame. ... What is surprising, and is not widely recognized, is the extent to which these creative communities are destructive. (2009)

In other words, the communities draw in precisely those individuals most likely to be able to see beyond the limits of the current worldview. But once inside, their talents are inexorably turned towards refining its structure rather than examining the limits of that structure. This provides a first class explanation of another Kuhn dictum:

> Those who achieve fundamental inventions of a new paradigm have generally been either very young or very new to the field whose paradigm they changed. (1962, 90)

Normal Science

Kuhn defines 'normal science' as working within the community to refine the structure of the existing paradigm in the existing theories. This is the landscape of knowledge within which the scientists of the day operate, more or less exclusively. As he states:

> No part of the aim of normal science is to call forth new sorts of phenomenon; indeed those that will not fit the box are often not seen at all. (1962, 24)

They are not looking for truly novel solutions because these inevitably lie outside the domain of the current paradigm. So although anomalies are inevitably discovered, these are swept under the carpet as acceptable levels of error. Or, if they are too potentially intrusive, simply ignored. Shut up and calculate! Thus scientific revolutions are always breakdowns of the ordinary business of normal science.

Experience Denied

Changizi's explanation reveals the roots of the stasis that has kept our scientific worldview stuck in the classical age. Truly novel solutions are proscribed. As a result, the radical breakthroughs that resolve the great paradoxes in the two pillars of the new physics are resolutely ignored. In quantum theory, Hugh Everett's famous many-worlds resolves the central paradox, the measurement problem, but his explanation hinges on the axiomatic relevance of experience. In relativity, the paradox of the passage of time is explained by the core significance of the experiencing consciousness, as Hermann Weyl explains. Both these new insights are inadmissible because the subjective perspective is rigorously debarred from consideration. And the stasis is so complete that this has gone unquestioned for over half a century.

The paradoxes have defied all attempts to explain them from within the current paradigm because there is no route forward to the solutions starting with the physical world. As demonstrated in the text, only when we take Everett and Weyl at face value and follow the logic from there do we find a natural path to the solutions. The breakthroughs have remained incomprehensible because they arise from fundamental category errors that require stepping outside of the current paradigm in order to see the nature of the problems.

III

Quantum Bayesianism

'Bayesian probability' is a long-standing technical method of calculating probabilities in everyday situations. Its use in a successful search for a lost sea vessel is a famous example. 'Quantum Bayesianism', now known as QBism, is a new interpretation of quantum theory that applies this technique to probabilities in quantum mechanics. Physicist Christopher Fuchs is the main author. With his colleagues he has shown that applying this approach to quantum theory resolves the longstanding paradoxes. This is the power of QBism.

QBism Reality

QBism arrives at the same position as the Copenhagen interpretation, the first explanation of quantum theory. There is no objective reality. Only what is observed is determinate, and all else is unreal. As the physicist Niels Bohr, the main author, famously declared:

> There is no quantum world. There is only an abstract quantum physical description. (Petersen, 1963)

In other words, the quantum wave function is the only definition of physical reality there is. And since the wave function is a wave of probability, probability is all there is. This is described in detail in Part 2. This concept is heavily supported by the big discovery in QBism. The paradoxical behaviour of matter and energy fundamental to quantum mechanics is actually defined by Bayesian probability.

Bayesian Probability

What is Bayesian probability? The science of probabilities goes back centuries, using basic methods of counting how frequently something specific happens. This is called 'frequentist' probability. A coin toss with a fair coin should come up heads half the time and tails half the time. A loaded coin is detected by doing a large number of tosses, and a significant deviation from fifty-fifty is the giveaway. In many situations, however, estimates of the odds of a situation are needed in circumstances where there is no history of similar events available. Then we have to use Bayesian probability.

Bayesian probability is a well-established technique that is more sophisticated. It is based on weighting the existing data of related events observed in the past. Frequencies are included if available. This data is then analysed for relevance to possible events and situations in the future to calculate a probability. For instance, the reputation of the owner of the coin is all part of such an assessment.

QBism

QBism has achieved a remarkable breakthrough. As described by von Baeyer (2013, 51), Fuchs has shown that Bayesian probability, determined solely by subjective observations, provides a precise match with the 'Born rule'. This is the law that defines the probabilistic definition of the outcome of events in quantum mechanics.[8] The massive question is why. How can we understand what this means? As philosopher of physics Simon Saunders poses the question:

> ... why should subjective probability track chance? (2004, 2)

In other words, why on Earth should events observed in life conceivably affect the probabilities of events in quantum experiments?

---

8 This is akin to the way the math Einstein needed to make relativity work was already present in Lorenz mechanics. Special relativity theory was originally called the Lorentz-Einstein theory. Logic and math generated in one context turn out to be exactly applicable in another field.

The answer is that both domains are defined by exactly the same information. Bayesian probability is the deduction of the probabilities of future events from past observations. Highly counter-intuitive though it is, the physical reality itself is also defined solely by past observations. This is the central point of QBism: only what is observed is determinate. The full explanation is given in Part 2.

The key point, and the major departure from the universally accepted worldview in modern physics, is that experience is fundamental:

> Although it differs in many important ways from what has come to be called "the Copenhagen interpretation", QBism — Quantum Bayesianism — agrees with Bohr that the primitive concept of experience is fundamental to an understanding of science. (Fuchs et al., 2013, 1)

The idea of experience being fundamental is almost universally rejected in modern physics, so QBism is not taken seriously.

The implications are even more of an anathema. It means that different people have different versions of the real world; the authors' quote is given on page 14. The resistance to such ideas is deep and widespread, but in fact this concept follows directly from the basics of quantum theory. This is the meaning of the thought experiment of 'Wigner's friend' as described in Chapter 27. And there is now supporting evidence from physical experiment, as cited in the Preface.

It means that each person has a different definition of the probable future of the world. The differences may be small, but in the complexity of the world in which the beat of a butterfly's wing may redirect a tornado as chaos theory demonstrates, they can diverge greatly.

The World is Real

As QBism shows, the only world that fits all the facts is one that is indeterminate where unobserved. The authors take this to mean that there *is* no objective reality 'out there', another reason why

QBism is so roundly rejected. But this is wrong. The ordinary world is every bit as real as we take it to be. This is indeed the basis of all physical reality, just as seems totally obvious. The key is that both perspectives are correct. The beauty of the new paradigm described here is that we do not need to give up the objective world, quite the opposite. The standard concept of the ordinary world is perfectly correct, but the QBism world is correct also. As described in Chapter 7, it is just a different view of the same universe.

Two Types of Worlds

The objective world of the current scientific worldview, the quasi-classical world, is the basis of all reality as is obvious. But the world subjectively encountered is a completely different kind of thing, a holographic universe. This is the effect of the QBism world as described in the text. It is determinate only where experienced as QBism holds. It is this kind of world that is idiosyncratic to each person.

As described in Appendix I, the scientific worldview does not change unless there is valid alternative. In QBism there is no such thing as objective physical reality, and thus it is not considered as such. The explanation of the holographic universe presented here makes it clear that there is nothing wrong with the well-established concept of the objective physical reality. The new worldview does not contradict the existing paradigm but just extends it.

A major concern has been that the basic framework of modern physics might be inadequate or even wrong. The new worldview presented here means that the great paradoxes are resolved while at the same time the current worldview is confirmed as essentially correct. The quasi-classical world is the objective physical reality. The holographic universe is the physical reality subjectively encountered.

IV

Altering Reality

In *Changing the Past by Forgetting* (2009) physicist Saibal Mitra presents the basic physics of changing reality dramatically, in effect, just by altering an observation. The many-worlds interpretation is assumed. The physics applies equally to interactive destiny.

Dodging Armageddon

In Mitra's thought experiment an individual makes an observation both massively unlikely and hugely unwelcome, a planet-killing asteroid heading straight for his world. Bizarrely, however, if he deletes the memory of this observation, he is thereby back in the kind of reality he was in before, in which doomsday asteroids are fantastically unlikely. In other words, this is the reality undo most of us have longed for on occasions. This is not because he has changed the objective physical reality, of course, but because he is now present in a different version of physical reality. He is in a different 'sector of the multiverse' as Mitra phrases it. If he looks through the telescope in this different version of the world, the chances he will see a massive asteroid bearing down on him are next to zero.

Mitra demonstrates this concept in the technical terms of quantum physics equations, but the effect can be very easily explained in terms of the concepts described here. When the observation is deleted, the individual is then defined as existing in a different version of the superworld, with a different future. This is the superposition of all the worlds in which there is no record of the observation being made. Naturally, this includes the world in which the observation was made, and was then deleted. And in this world, of course, the asteroid is still on its way. But the vast majority of the worlds in the new version of his superworld define no such perilous situation. So the new, *overall* probability of dangerous asteroids in this superworld is of regular, very low probability.

Humans cannot do this kind of thing because we cannot delete memory in this way. Memory is only lost in that it degrades. It is a holistic system. We can only add memories. We cannot forget deliberately. The individual in Mitra's thought experiment is an artificial intelligence like Mr Data in Star Trek. For him this would be a real operation he could perform at any time. (But it *only* works for him, so Mr Data could not save the rest of the crew from a catastrophic mishap.)

Although we cannot delete memories, the thought experiment is useful in understanding how interactive destiny works. When the unconscious modifies an observation before it is added to memory, this effectively changes the superworld in just the same kind of way. The superworld now includes all the worlds in which the preferred version of the observation was actually made, in reality. But the physical reality is of course unchanged. So the superworld also contains worlds in which the observation was altered before being recorded. But the new overall probability of the future is different.

The overall effect is to alter the probabilities of events in the future of this individual's personal world. This is described in more detail in Appendix V. Common sense cries out that this cannot be the case, but our common sense is based on the ordinary flying-rock world, and as philosopher of physics David Wallace dryly states:

> Our intuitions about what is "reasonable" or "imaginable" were designed to aid our ancestors on the savannahs of Africa, and the universe is not obliged to conform to them. (2011, 17)

V

Strange Attractors

Confirmation bias is a purely internal process, triggered by expectation, but in the QBism type of world the alteration of observations changes which version of the future this individual is likely to experience. The fulfilment of the expectations becomes increasingly likely. So in technical terms, expectations act as 'strange attractors'. This means that the system tends to gravitate toward the fulfilment of the expectations. This is the effect of interactive destiny.

Attractors

In physics, the term 'attractor' means a state towards which a system tends to gravitate. Gravity itself is the classic example. A ball dropped on a slope tends to roll towards the bottom. Because of gravity the bottom of the hill is an attractor for things that roll. Another simple example of an attractor is the way a cup of tea cools to room temperature. The temperature of the environment is an attractor for the temperature of any object because all objects tend to cool down, or warm up, to the temperature of the surroundings.

In both these examples the attractor is obvious in the way it works, and the end result is a specific condition: the ball at the bottom of the slope, the cup of tea at room temperature. There is also a rather different sort of attractor that is often found in complex systems, a strange attractor. This sort of attractor does not give rise to a simple, specific outcome, but a loosely defined tendency in the system. Rather than one specific outcome, a strange attractor gives rise to a particular pattern of behaviour in the system. The Lorenz attractor shown in Figure V is a well-known example from mathematics. This is a pattern traced out by a mathematical formula in a program on a computer. The program traces out a shape that always gravitates towards this distinctive pattern. The shape of the pattern is a strange attractor.

Interactive Destiny

Expectations act as strange attractors because the resulting confirmation bias induces tendencies in the system of the personal world. This is not just because one behaves in such a way as to fulfil the expectation, though for some local events, of course, that may well be going on. Firstly, what we expect to see in and of itself alters the process of observation as has now been demonstrated in research:

> Our findings provide compelling evidence that visual working memory representations directly interact with the same neural mechanisms as those involved in processing basic sensory events. (Kang et al., 2011)

This causes confirmation bias when observations of basic sensory events are altered by what one has in the mind's eye. Thus probabilities are biased toward their fulfilment being experienced. Suppose

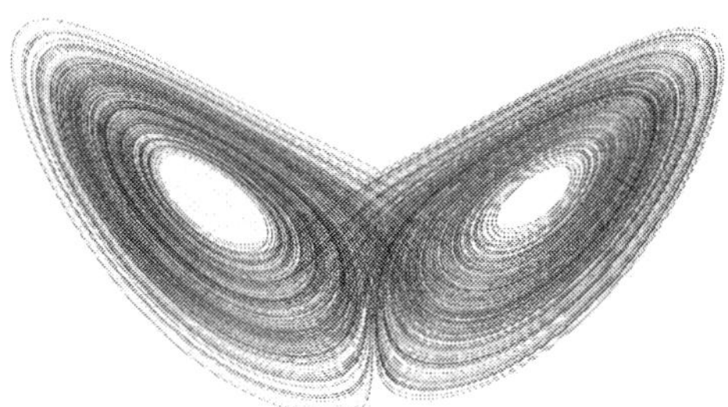

Figure V The Lorenz attractor.
It can be seen in action at https://en.wikipedia.org/wiki/Lorenz_system.

you have been looking forward to an event. Then you go past the notice board where it is listed, and it has a cancelled notice across the bottom; but your picture of the future overrides the meaning of the sensory input, and instead you see a confirmation notice. Your superworld now contains all the worlds in which you observed the confirmation notice. So you have unconsciously made a jump into a version of the world where it is confirmed the event is going ahead.

But of course your superworld also contains worlds in which it is cancelled, and your confirmation bias worked to make you see it wrong. Your superworld now includes both versions of the world. So the net result in the reality of your superworld is indeterminate, but clearly the overall probability of seeing the event has been increased.

This illustrates the world of QBism. The likely future is defined solely by all the past observations of life experience, hence Bayesian as described in Appendix III. If you see the same thing when you go back to check, the Bayesian probability is greatly increased.

The whole thing seems utterly incredible from within our current worldview, but the superworld in which one lives is very different. It is a holographic universe that operates exactly as described in QBism. As the authors clearly state, quoted in Chapter 3, what is real for an agent rests entirely on what that agent experiences. This means that if confirmation bias causes a different version of an event to be experienced, the physical reality of this individual is different as a result. The probabilities of future events are altered, and the individual is more likely to encounter a version of the world in which the expectation is fulfilled. The physics of how this operates is described in detail in Chapter 28.

VI

Quantum Mysticism

There have been various ludicrous claims attributed to quantum theory in order to explain spiritual and religious beliefs. Quantum mysticism is a derogatory term often applied in this context. Given certain scientists' motivation described in Appendix VII, the strong desire to get rid of God, one can see the motive for dismissing all such things without reserve. But with respect to consciousness the baby gets thrown out with the bathwater. The idea of consciousness being relevant to the physics is now generally considered absolutely ridiculous, but this means that how reality actually works is incomprehensible.

Fantastic Reality

As described in Chapter 10, the word consciousness is used indiscriminately for two very different types of phenomena, and the muddled amalgam is routinely taken to be nothing but a property of the brain. Weyl, of course, is using the word in the sense of the phenomenal consciousness, the experiencing itself. As described in Chapter 17 this is a third-logical-type phenomenon. And this explains how reality actually works.

So mystics get the last laugh. But the main point here is that we may do well not to judge revolutionary ideas as nonsense just because they greatly resemble some fantastic myth. It turns out that the nature of reality *is* fantastic, but it is also perfectly rational and scientific once the triune ontology of logical types is taken into account. The physical reality in which one lives is a personal superworld, a kind of solipsism, and in this kind of domain certain myths that sound fantastic are just how the world actually works.

Interactive destiny is a real phenomenon, and thus visualisation is unreasonably effective. So prayer actually works. Any kind of visualisation induces strange attractors, though involving a deity may or may not be helpful. Karma operates, but again this is nothing to do with deity, it is just how the superworld operates. The new paradigm also means that the Holy Trinity is perfectly real, as described in Appendix VII, but not exactly as usually understood. Furthermore, the nature of the experiencing consciousness means we are immortal. As Moravec describes, death cannot be the end. All this is certainly fantastic, but this is simply the reality of the new physics taken at face value.

Mysticism, meaning gaining insight into ultimate or hidden truths, is of vital importance. It is the great mystics who produced the user manual for this type of reality, where not only actions but intentions matter. As described in Chapter 13 this is the Noble Eightfold Path of Buddhism. The Ten Commandments form the quick start guide. These principles are absolutely essential, not only for us to do well personally but also for our race to live long and prosper.

It is from mysticism that the understanding of the higher self arises. As a world hologram, experienced by universe consciousness, you are a child of the universe, and your expectations are active and efficacious in your personal physical reality, worldwide. You are the pilot of your holographic universe. As the wise have been known to say, be careful what you wish for.

VII

The God Concept

Certain of the greatest myths are borne out in the new paradigm. You are immortal because consciousness always continues. Thus the world hologram spans lifetimes. This is the soul. Karma is explained by the results of strange attractors, as is the unreasonable effectiveness of visualisations. One would expect prayer to work. Heaven and hell are just the different types of reincarnation that different karmas produce. These are not just lucky guesses by our ancestors. As stated by the philosopher Gilbert Ryle, quoted on page 78, a myth is not a fairytale, but rather a misallocation of facts that belong in a different category of knowledge. In other words, these great myths, common to so many traditions, are real attributes of reality expressed in the idioms of folklore. This is just how the seemingly inexplicable truths of natural science were made somewhat more accessible.

In this chapter the Holy Trinity is shown to be an anthropomorphism of the triune ontology of operational reality, at the three levels of logical type. On this view the myth is essentially true, but the meaning is not quite the same as in the traditional folk-tale.

Traditionally, God is thought of as eternal, omniscient, omnipotent, omnipresent and of divine simplicity, an almighty, perfect person. This is what I believed in as an imaginative small child raised Christian. For the faithful there is an understanding this is a real and active phenomenon in the world. We could not be more right. What is seldom acknowledged is the role played by the individual.

The Trinity of the Whole

As Bishop John Spong states in *Why Christianity Must Change or Die*, God is simply the universe itself:

> God is not a being superior to all other beings. He is the Ground of Being itself. (1998, 70)

It just is. It is not a person. It is the totality of existence. This defines the first, primitive, logical type, the quantum state of physical reality. Provided it is not taken to be a person, the myth of God the Father is clearly valid. It is the 'parent' in that it is the origin of all being, meaning that from which everything arises. God the Mother, the fundamental Matrix, meaning that from which everything is formed and within which everything is laid out, fits even better.

Consciousness is a fundamental property of this totality. As described in Chapter 17, it is universe consciousness, the third-logical-type phenomenon that breathes life into the equations of physics. This corresponds precisely to God the Holy Spirit. Spirit means that which brings to life. This is the spirit of the totality, of the whole – the original meaning of holy. This is not a person either. It is life itself. As described in Chapter 20, it has no character of any kind. It is literally the Holy Ghost, a property of the entirety, utterly present, utterly vital, but invisible and intangible. This is the causal phenomenon of the universe itself, the origin of all experiential and transtemporal reality.

Consciousness experiences the physical world through the medium of the world hologram. The result, of course, *is* a person, a conscious individual. In technical terms this is literally a child process. Each one is brought into existence by the interaction of the Spirit with the Matrix, the experience of a specific physical entity by consciousness. Each one is a holographic movie of life, a soul, a second-logical-type phenomenon. This completes the trinity of logical types.

Notably, this trinity of fundamental types is recognised in the Gnosticism of early Christianity. As stated by biblical scholar Jim West:

> Tertullian's description of the Gnostic "trinity" shows no connection with the three persons but instead refers to a doctrine of three natures. What Tertullian actually describes is a Gnostic doctrine which maintains that the universe is comprised of three fundamental substances or natures, which are identified as spirit, soul and matter. (2009)

Here the principle underlying the anthropomorphisms is recognised, the triune ontology itself.

So there is a God the Father/Mother, an almighty physical totality, in that it is imposing and awesome, but it is static. It is what is. There is a God the Holy Ghost, which is the dynamic experience that brings to life this unchanging almighty, the gaze of universe consciousness. The genesis of the world hologram, the soul, fits as God the Child, a product of the two. Each individual is a world hologram, instantiated in the physical, experienced by universe consciousness. This is why the individual seems a bit godlike, being immortal and at cause, but only in one's own holographic universe.

God is Real

God as a superior being, both almighty and interested in humanity, is an archetype, a vision of perfection. The deity one acknowledges as God is an avatar of the archetype. This God becomes active in human reality because this is a powerful strange attractor.

When mental images and expectations are formed, interactive destiny operates. The strange attractors that are generated progressively increase the probability of observing events and circumstances that are in accord with the character of the archetype. Thus to follow the correct practices is to initialise strange attractors that make it increasingly likely that appropriate events will increasingly be experienced, especially if prayer and ceremony are involved. These practices induce belief and expectation – that is their operational purpose. Inevitably, therefore, the experience of events apparently confirming the existence of the archetypal entity in one way or another happens more and more: there is positive feedback. Thus the principles embodied become more and more real in the world encountered. The avatar is increasingly ensouled, meaning that in operational terms it becomes increasingly real. Potentially this leads to experiential evidence of what is then taken to be indubitable truth. The experiences and insights are recorded for posterity. Scriptures are written.

God as an all-powerful being that cares for us is a superpotent archetype because this is inescapably associated with the parents of early life. Thus qualities such as authority and love are automatically projected onto it. As Richard Dawkins states:

> There is something infantile in the presumption that somebody else (parents in the case of children, God in the case of adults) has a responsibility to give your life meaning and point. (2006, 404)

The truth seldom addressed is that to the degree it is personified it cannot be anything other than personal. As many religions have made clear in different ways, the Tao that can be told is not the eternal Tao. An anthropomorphic deity is a 'graven image' in the mind, a feature of the world hologram of the individual. So in psychological terms this is a projection. But in this context it is none the less real for that. It is ensouled, meaning it can generate thoughts and actions. This is all part of the structure of your karma. This is what determines what is likely in the future of your holographic universe. God is real.

The great problem is that it is not understood for what it is, and the results have been catastrophic. Physicist Paul Davies even states that:

> Many scientists who are struggling to construct a fully comprehensible theory of the physical universe openly admit that part of the motivation is to finally get rid of God, whom they view as a dangerous and infantile delusion. (2006b, 16)

By this I am sure these people do not wish to deny the possibility of spiritual truths, or opportunities for self-development that do not stop at the purely mundane. The dangerous and infantile elements of religion are not based in seeking the spiritual but in the belief in an all-seeing, all-powerful God with a narcissistic, child-level psychology, the very opposite of an ideal parent God. Appalling consequences have arisen from the requirements of such a God being enacted by human cultures.

In the holographic universe, only that which has been observed is determinate, and everything else is to some degree indeterminate. By definition, dogma is not determined by any observations. Ironically therefore, the claim that a dogma is definitely true is by definition false.

Evidence

As has been shown, certain great myths turn out to be fundamental principles of reality, expressed in the idioms of more primitive cultures. These principles emerge from the experimental evidence and accepted scientific fact, a body of knowledge that is all based exclusively on observations that are extensively researched and properly documented. But it is only these principles that are confirmed.

And I wish to record that I am delving into these highly emotive subjects with considerable reluctance, and I apologise wholeheartedly for any offence, but it seems absolutely essential not to leave a tempting tabula rasa at the heart of the new paradigm.

I believe that this is good news for everyone, not least for the deeply devout. Nothing is lost, and the path is open. The ordinary individual is a far cry from the higher self, the soul that is identified with the whole. To align with this identity means to appreciate interactive destiny and karma, and to acknowledge the inherent morality. It means taking the long-term view of the immortal. Such individuals are empowered and responsible, and live for the benefit of all as best they may. This is true religion in the literal sense, meaning reconnection with the whole of oneself and the awesome enormity of life.

VIII

Decoherence

The wave function of the universe defines all physical possibilities. 'Quantum decoherence' is what transforms the wave function into specific versions of physical reality. This is an interference effect that alters the structure of the wave function, producing essentially classical states. This is what transforms the amorphous fundamental wave function into an ordinary world of the sort we are used to.

It has been proposed that this phenomenon resolves the whole problem of the collapse of the wave function. But as stated by physicist Guido Bacciagaluppi in *The Role of Decoherence in Quantum Mechanics*, such claims are part of the naïve folklore of decoherence which "... deservedly attract the wrath of physicists and philosophers alike." (2012). In any case, this cannot be the whole story because different observers would be in the same physical environment on that basis, and as shown by the experimental confirmation of the Wigner's friend concept by Proietti et al. (2019) they are not.

Entanglement

Physicist Sean Carroll argues that quantum entanglement, i.e. decoherence, solves the measurement problem:

> The Many-Worlds formulation of quantum mechanics removes once and for all any mystery about the measurement process and collapse of the wave function. ... there's nothing special about what constitutes 'a measurement' or 'an observ-

er' – a measurement is any interaction that causes a quantum system to become entangled with the environment, creating a branching into separate worlds, and an observer is any system that brings about such an interaction. Consciousness, in particular, has nothing to do with it. (2019)

This is a perfectly valid argument for physical entities, but an inescapable consequence is that observers are all in the same physical world. But as described in Chapter 27, experimental confirmation of Wigner's friend shows us that conscious individuals live in different versions of physical reality. As Bacciagaluppi describes in detail in his article, although it has been popular to suggest that physical correlations resolve the paradox of the measurement problem, this simply does not work. Furthermore, the paradox of the 'preferred basis' problem is unresolved. As described in Appendix IX, this means that the basis on which decoherence operates in this context cannot be determined.

Decoherence served to produce the quasi-classical worlds of the many-worlds universe, but they are all present and superposed. These are the classical parallel worlds described on page 88. But the whole thing is still one 'world' as Cox describes. As Everett states, although all the possible versions of the world do happen, it is only in experience that one single, specific version of the world exists.

So the phenomenon that Carroll describes is certainly in operation, but this cannot be the complete answer. When it comes to explaining Wigner's friend, only Everett's stated solution works. His formulation is described in Chapter 22. The resolution is the fundamental dualism of types of frame of reference, inside-view and outside-view, as described in Appendix IX . This is what resolves the paradox of Wigner-'s friend, the preferred basis problem and the measurement problem.

IX

The Preferred Basis

Along with the measurement problem, the preferred basis problem presents a major stumbling block to the understanding of quantum theory. The challenge is to define basis of physical reality. In this context the basis means the fundamental terms in which physical reality is defined. The preferred basis is the one in some sense 'preferred' by nature.

It seems obvious that the basis of physical reality is the components of physical matter, but it is not quite as simple as that. Exactly which properties of matter? As philosopher of physics Jeffrey Barrett quips:

> Making the total angular momentum of all the sheep in Austria determinate by choosing such a preferred basis to tell us when worlds split, would presumably do little to account for the determinate memory I have concerning what I just typed. But this is the problem, we do not really know what basis would make our most immediately accessible physical records, those records that determine our experiences and beliefs, determinate in every world. The problem of choosing which observable to make determinate is known as the preferred-basis problem. (2008)

As he states, the acid test is that the correct basis has to give a specific determinate state to the records that determine our experiences, i.e. the world hologram. And the problem is that no ordinary physical basis works. The angular momentum of the Austrian sheep population does not work, but neither does *anything* physical.

The Consciousness Basis

Clearly, there is a phenomenon that is making everyone's experiences determinate. But what is the basis actually in operation, the basis that nature apparently 'prefers', the basis on which the specific determinate world we witness is actually being defined?

The simple but radical solution is to take the records that determine our experiences *as* the preferred basis. This is the explanation given by Lockwood (1989) in his many-minds theory, which is described in Appendix XIII. This takes the central significance of experience at face value. But what is the rationale? It seems obvious that just looking at objects can hardly be the cause of the splitting of worlds. This, however, is exactly the case – on the inside view.

The reason is that the world of the inside view is not just an ordinary quasi-classical world but a superworld. And in this physical frame of reference the determinacy is defined by observations, as has been described. And the physical reality of the inside view splits with the making of each observation because the different outcomes give rise to different world holograms. The result is the emergence of different versions of reality, as illustrated in Figure 22.1. These are the different relative states. Thus on the inside view, observation, experience, is the preferred basis, meaning the one actually in action. Lockwood calls this the consciousness basis. This is the approach taken in QBism, and as the authors demonstrate this fits the physics perfectly.

The nature of consciousness helps to explain this. On the inside view the world hologram is the basis because this is literally the basis on which consciousness encounters physical reality. The world hologram is what consciousness actually experiences. As Lockwood states this: "... in a sense is the primary observable" (1996, 185), by which he means the quantum-mechanical basis, that which defines reality. This means that the superposition of worlds to form the superworld is inevitable, as described in Appendix XIII. To the view of consciousness, ubiquitous and omnipresent, all copies of the world hologram are one.

The Physical Basis

This is not the whole story either, however. As Tegmark states, location and other classical features form the natural basis:

> Decoherence also explains why states resembling classical physics have special status: they are the most robust to decoherence. (2007)

The basic principles of physics bring this about. As he explains:

> Essentially, the position basis gets singled out by the dynamics because the field equations of physics are local in this basis, not in any other basis. (1997, 3)

So objectively, the preferred basis is physical position, just as intuition naturally suggests. This is obviously the basis on which ordinary realities like ours are defined and laid out. Quite right, there is nothing wrong with the physics. The key point is that the basis in operation is different on outside and inside views. This is the resolution of the preferred basis problem. What it actually means is that there is a fundamental dualism. This is the meaning of quantum mechanics.

The Dualism of Bases

On the outside view the world operates just as Carroll describes. The basis on which the world is defined is physical. Physical interactions cause branching. But on the inside view the basis is experience. As described in Part 1, the physical reality of the inside view, the superworld, is determinate solely where defined by experiences, and all else is indeterminate, thus it changes as each observation is made.

There is a fundamental, ontological difference between the physical realities of objective and subjective views. On the outside view the world is the quasi-classical world, and the basis is the classical-physics properties of the ordinary world. Thus the quasi-classical world is an ordinary physical domain just as we imagine it to be – a cosmos of real solid stuff made of matter and energy. But the basis of the reality *experienced*, the physical reality of the inside view, the superworld, is the observations recorded to form the world hologram.

We know that both perspectives are correct. The physical basis gives rise to the quasi-classical world of modern physics, as our instruments detect it. The consciousness basis gives rise to the world of the inside view, as is universally experienced, and experiment shows that this kind of world is indeterminate where unobserved. This means that a dualism of bases is the only rational conclusion. It means there is a dualism of 'unilateral relative onticities' as described in Appendix XVI.

Once again, the solution is simply taking the physics at face value even though the result is radical. There is a dualism of fundamental types of physical reality, at two different levels of logical type. These are the physical realities of inside and outside views, and their bases are fundamentally different.

The paradox of the incompatible dynamics of quantum mechanics, the famous measurement problem, is the direct evidence of this dualism. As described in Appendix XII, the two different quantum-mechanical dynamics operate exclusively in these two different types of frame of reference. Their cyclical operation is illustrated in Chapter 28.

X

The Relative State

Everett titled his theory *'Relative-State' Formulation of Quantum Mechanics*. It means that the quantum state of the world that the individual encounters exists *only* relative to that individual. And this means that quantum theory is exactly like relativity, in that fundamental properties of the world are not absolute – they exist only relative to the specific individual.

Correlations

When Everett states that a subsystem does not have an independent existence, it means that there is no determinate definition of the physical reality of the individual except as defined by the observations of this individual. This explains why physical reality is 'observer-dependent', meaning different for different people, as in Wigner's friend. Correlations are central to the explanation.

A correlation between two systems simply means that something that is true about one subsystem is also true about the other. It is an inevitable consequence that observations of a system generate correlations between the observed and the observer. The information gained means that the observer has information about the observed. And this means that the state of the memory of the observer, and the state of the observed entity, have this information in common. So the correlation is just the direct and immediate effect of the observation being made. This is what Everett means by correlations:

> ... all measurement and observation processes are to be regarded simply as interactions between observer and object-system which produce strong correlations. (1973, 10)

> The mathematics leads one to recognize the concept of the relativity of states, in the following sense: a constituent subsystem cannot be said to be in any single well-defined state, independently of the remainder of the composite system. ... Thus the state of one subsystem does not have an independent existence, but is fixed only by the state of the remaining subsystem. In other words, the states occupied by the subsystems are not independent, but *correlated*. (1957, 455)

Observer-Dependent

The nature of the superworld explains how correlations in terms of sensory data become ontic. The superworld is determinate only where defined by the record of observations, and the observations define the correlations. Thus the determinacy of the superworld in which one lives, and the domain on which physics experiments are carried out, is defined solely by the correlations of sensory data. This is the relative state, the observer-dependent world. Experimental evidence has now been demonstrated in the confirmation of the Wigner's friend concept, as described in Chapter 27. The cosmology is the holographic universe.

The only absolutely fundamental reality, that which is real in all circumstances, is the universe of all possible worlds. This is what Everett calls the absolute state. But the absolute state is the famous 'view from nowhere'. This is the theoretical view from 'outside' of the universe, the system as a whole, that does not have an outside. The real physical world encountered by any given individual is the world of the inside view. The result is multi-solipsism. It means we live in personal, physical, parallel realities, idiosyncratic holographic universes. That is how the universe works at this level of logical type.

XI

Experiencing the Wave Function

This appendix explains how consciousness brings the world to life, resulting in the enactment of both of the two dynamics of quantum mechanics, linear and collapse, in the static block universe.

The Paradox

The viewpoint of any observer moves through space-time at the speed of light. This is fundamental to relativity. A good explanation of how we know this, along with some of the very strange implications, is given by the theoretical physicist and mathematician Brian Greene in his book *The Elegant Universe* (1999, 26), with excellent illustrations. But *why* this is happening is a total mystery. There is no explanation of how anything could possibly move or change in the static block universe that relativity defines. As stated by philosopher Rebecca Goldstein, the universe defined by relativity is static, a permanent and eternal, four-dimensional, space-time existence:

> In Einstein's physics, there is no passage of time, no unidirectional flow from the fixed past and toward the uncertain future. The temporal component of space-time is as static as its spatial components; physical time is as still as physical space. It is all laid out, the whole spread of events, in the tenseless four-dimensional space-time manifold. (2005, 254)

So how does physical reality actually work? There is a simple solution as Weyl describes. The viewpoint of the experiencing consciousness passes through time. That gives the experience of time passing, and thus the enactment of the dynamics. But how does *that* work? The answer goes to the essence of the experiencing consciousness.

Linear

The wave function is the fundamental definition of physical reality. The linear dynamics is the time evolution of physical reality that is defined by the wave function. The wave function is a function in the mathematical sense. For instance, MPH, Miles Per Hour, is literally the speed function, meaning the function defining the relationship between distance and time. The number of miles covered is a function of the hours spent travelling. The wave function defines how the fundamental components of reality, the quanta, change as time progresses. Thus, as the linear dynamics operates, quanta move and interact, things happen and the world changes. But time does not progress. The universe is static. Thus, as physicist Paul Davies suggests, quoted in Chapter 19, the flow of time is subjective. Here it is proposed that this is literally true, meaning that the experience *of* the wave function is the experience of it functioning.

In the progression of the linear dynamics, the positions and other attributes of the fundamental components of reality change. Thus the configuration of the world corresponds to later and later times. In other words, the viewpoint is defined as further and further along the worldline into the future. Thus effectively, on the inside view, there is the passage of time. Thus to experience the wave function that defines this linear dynamics is to experience passing through time. This is the experience of the viewpoint being defined as further and further along the worldline into the future. Effectively, in the subjectively defined holographic universe, the world gets older.

Subjective experience that has no correlate in physical reality is the experience of 'qualia'. As philosopher Thomas Nagel said, "... there is something it is like" (1974) to experience the smell of a rose in bloom.

Qualia

These subjective attributes are the essence of experience, but pass unnoticed as such. As the cognitive scientist Daniel Dennett states:

> "Qualia" is an unfamiliar term for something that could not be more familiar to each of us: the *ways things seem to us*. (1988, Abstract)

One of the central points made by both Chalmers and Ned Block (1995), another philosopher specialising in consciousness, is that the subjective qualities of experience, the qualia, cannot be explained in purely objective physical terms. In other words, it seems that qualia are a further category to existence, inexplicable in terms of physics or biology. In the new paradigm the explanation is easy. This is what it is like for universe consciousness to experience reality.

The deeply familiar sense we all have of the passage of time is what it is like for consciousness to experience the wave function, functioning. And as a result the linear dynamics is experienced in action. This gives rise to the experience of the passage of time. If you are experiencing speed, you are experiencing your location in space constantly changing at a certain rate. That is what it is like. Time passing is what it is like to experience the wave function of physical reality: the location in time is constantly changing at a certain rate: at light speed, as is fundamental to relativity. In effect time passes. And we all get older.

Collapse

The collapse dynamics is a completely different type of process. As described in Chapter 17, this is a process that takes place purely in the superworld of the individual. As the linear dynamics progresses, the observer makes the next observation. When this occurs, the world hologram changes, and this changes the definition of the class of worlds in which this world hologram is instantiated. The superworld is redefined. And this means that the physical reality of this individual is defined by a different wave function. If this is me turning round to see the butterfly, I now live in a reality where his wings have a specific determinate position. This is the experience of the collapse dynamics in operation. This process is described in detail in Chapter 28. Again this is a purely subjective phenomenon. So both dynamics operate only subjectively, in experience.

The Real Appearance

All this explains why the appearance of both dynamics in action actually happens, while in actuality no such processes take place in physical reality. There is the appearance of the passage of time as Weyl describes because this is the experiencing of the wave function by consciousness, and thus the linear dynamics is effectively enacted. There is the appearance of events happening and the world changing as Everett describes because this is the experience of the viewpoint passing from one version of the physical world to the next. This is what it is like to experience the change of the definition of physical reality on the inside view.

This is why one encounters the appearance of the passage of time, and the world changing, even though the universe itself is static. But this is not an illusion as has often been suggested, meaning a false mental image, a seeming phenomenon where there is really no such thing. On the inside view these are real phenomena, just as seems obvious. This is how the world actually works. The meaning is deeply counterintuitive in the science of physics because it only works subjectively, in experience. The virtual nature of the operation of the physical reality is described in more detail in Appendix XVII.

XII

The Measurement Problem

> The measurement problem arises from the fact that the standard theory's two dynamical laws are incompatible: one is linear and the other nonlinear. ... they constitute contradictory descriptions of the time-evolution of physical states (Barrett, 2011)

The resolution is that they operate at different levels of logical type, and the cycle of the two dynamics is the cycle of the holographic universe of the protagonist of both dynamics.

The Standard Formulation

In the standard formulation of quantum mechanics as given in textbooks, the two quantum-mechanical dynamics alternate in a cycle. This is the von Neumann-Dirac formulation of quantum mechanics (1932). Barrett provides a simplified form:

> Linear: If no observation is made, then the quantum system evolves continuously according to the linear, deterministic dynamics.
>
> Collapse: If an observation is made, then the quantum system instantaneously and randomly jumps to a state where it either determinately has or determinately does not have the property being observed. (2008; adapted)

As he also states, this is a superb theory, But as he goes on to explain, the theory seems inherently flawed:

> The standard theory ... is in one sense the most successful physical theory ever ... it successfully predicts the behaviour of the basic constituents of all physical things. (1999, 1)
>
> ... if one supposes that measuring devices are ordinary physical systems just like any other, constructed of fundamental particles interacting in their usual determinate way (and why wouldn't they be?), then the standard theory is logically inconsistent since no system can obey both the deterministic and stochastic dynamics simultaneously. This is the measurement problem. (1999, 15)

The usual determinate way to which he is referring is the linear dynamics, the dynamics of the wave function. This is a completely predictable, deterministic, sequential logic. The main point is that it gives rise to all possibilities in superposition. Since, Barrett is saying, the device used to make an observation can only be made of ordinary stuff, that operates according to the linear dynamics, it therefore *cannot* suddenly, randomly, come to exist in just one specific state as a result, and so define just one specific outcome to the observation. This is the measurement problem.

Dualism

The ontological physical dualism described in Chapter 17 is the solution. In the current paradigm it is automatically assumed that all the dynamics of the world, everything to do with physical reality, operate in a specific quasi-classical world. And in this case the measurement problem is insoluble, as a hundred years of study has demonstrated. But the two dynamics operate in two different types of frame of reference, at different levels of logical type. The linear dynamics operates within the context of the quasi-classical world. The collapse dynamics operates in the context of the class-of-worlds-as-a-world, the holographic universe of the mind.

They cycle as illustrated in Chapter 28. The time evolution of the linear dynamics operates within the context of a specific quantum state. This is experienced as the passage of time. When an observation made, that entire frame of reference changes. On the inside view the collapse of the wave function is encountered. This is what is experienced as events happening. The key point is that the effective operation of the collapse dynamics takes place in a domain 'outside', contextual to, the quasi-classical world. This operates at a higher level of logical type. It is the change of the class of world forming the holographic universe.

Understood as a dynamics of the class-of-worlds-as-a-world, this explains collapse on observation as a natural process. It is caused by the linear dynamics. It is in the progression of the linear dynamics that observations are made. On this inside view, and there alone, this alters the definition of the quantum state defining the wave function, with its linear dynamics. This effectively changes the quantum state and the linear dynamics defined by its wave function. This is the process of the collapse dynamics. It operates only on the inside view.

This dualism is the logical step that has been impossible to take within the bounds of physicalism. Only when we step outside do we find the new lexicon of logical types, the explanatory principle that has been missing. This is the basis of the fundamental ontological dualism in quantum theory that makes complete sense of the physics. There are two different types of definition of physical reality, at two different levels of logical type. Each operates its signature dynamics. That is the meaning of the measurement problem. The quasi-classical world operates the linear dynamics. The holographic universe defined by the superworld both follows the linear dynamics, and also operates the collapse dynamics.

XIII

Many Minds

In many-minds theories, different specific worlds exist only for a mind. As mathematician Matthew Donald introduces his theory:

> Many-minds interpretation of quantum mechanics extends the many-worlds interpretation by proposing that the distinction between worlds should be made at the level of the mind of an individual observer. (1998)

This is perfectly correct. The trouble is that these worlds have never been properly defined. The mind does indeed define the determinacy of the world but this only makes sense when it is a superworld.

The World 'Out There'

Though I got the logic, I always thought that many-minds theories were just too weird. As I soon discovered, this is a common view. The concept fits the facts, but how can the world be existing only as a mental phenomenon? QBism has the same problem. If only what is experienced is determinate, then there is no real world 'out there'. This is the direct implication of the Copenhagen interpretation, on which QBism is based. As Niels Bohr famously said, quoted on page 124, there is no quantum world. This is what makes these theories heavily contentious because this is so deeply counter to what we feel to be common sense. This time we are right. The *definition* of reality *is* all in your mind, but at the same time objective physical reality *is* 'out there'.

The world *encountered* is determinate only where defined by the world hologram, the mind, but this is because it is the superposed sum of a vast number of ordinary, physical, quasi-classical worlds: a class-of-worlds-as-a-world. And they are all perfectly real.

One of the central criticisms of the theory has been the lack of a satisfactory definition of the mind.[9] Here it is shown the Lockwood's definition corresponds precisely to the protagonist in Everett, here the world hologram. This shows that the logic is absolutely correct; what has been missing is the corresponding concept of the world. The great problem with the many-minds theories has been that the world it seems to describe clashes horribly with our common sense concept of the real world. It is so obviously an ordinary space-time domain as defined by the physics. Now we see that both are true.

The concepts presented here provide the ontology of Lockwood's theory, the explanation in terms of physical reality. The physical reality encountered is the superworld, and this is indeed defined by the mind. At the same time the objective quasi-classical world is entirely real. The quantum world is the space of all possible worlds. That is the absolute state. A superworld is a class of these worlds superposed.

This explains why the physics works as if there is nothing 'out there', while actually there is. All experiments are actually done in a superworld, where only what is observed is determinate, so it is exactly *as if* there is nothing 'out there', just as QBism suggests. But in fact the objective physical reality is all perfectly real. Thus the superworld provides a physical ontology for QBism, and of course the many-minds concept, that is entirely in accord with the current paradigm. Both types of world are real. This is described in detail in Appendix XVI. What has been missing is the explanation, the ontology.

---

9 In the first interpretation clearly stated as many-minds, Albert and Loewer (1988) suggested that different worlds exist only in the mind, but gave no definition of the mind. Donald (1998) defines the mind as the brain state plus the history of brain states. Lockwood (1996) defines the mind as the record of observations. Zeh (1970) refers to "many-perceptions".

Reality

Donald is also perfectly correct also in saying the world is largely indeterminate:

> Only the finite amount of information which determines one's structure as observer would determine the "world" in which one lives. (1997)

The observer here is of course the mind. This is the "observer" in Wiczek's statement in Chapter 29, the central protagonist of the physics that is missing from the current paradigm. As we have seen, the world hologram, the "observer", defines the determinacy of the physical environment.

A further level of explanation of the many-minds concept is provided by universe consciousness. From the point of view of the experiencing consciousness, the perceptual reality experienced is naturally the primary reality. The world hologram is what is directly experienced. In this context, *this* is the fundamental reality. As Lockwood states, quoted in Appendix IX, this is in a sense is the 'primary observable', meaning the fundamental basis of reality.

On this view the superposition of worlds that forms the superworld is inevitable. To the experiencing consciousness, inherently omnipresent, there is only one of a particular world hologram in the whole of existence. Thus the reality is inevitably the simultaneous experience of all the worlds in which it is instantiated, a superworld.

When only the finite amount of information defining the mind defines the determinacy of the world of each person as Donald proposes, the result is multi-solipsism. As stated in QBism, quoted in Chapter 3, reality is different for different people. This is the meaning of the many-minds interpretation. The superworld provides the ontology. We live in personal, physical, parallel realities, superworlds, overlapping holographic universes. Wigner's friend is the confirmation, as described in Chapter 27.

XIV

Missing Persons

As Mermin states in his article in *Nature* (2014), our worldview does not fit the facts, and the reason is that the conscious individual, the perceiving subject, has been omitted from the science. He could not be more right. The underlying reason is that the perceiving subject embodies the logical types missing from the pillars of the new physics.

The Perceiving Subject

As Mermin points out, the perceiving subject has been carefully excluded from the science, and this has led to the great paradoxes in both quantum theory and relativity. And thus the major, unrelated, long-standing problems are resolved when the subject is reinstated:

> In *Nature and the Greeks*, Austrian physicist Erwin Schrödinger traced the removal of the subject from science back more than two millennia. Alongside the spectacular success of physical science, this exclusion of personal experience has given rise to some vexing and persistent puzzles and paradoxes. ...
>
> The first problem is the notorious disagreement, confusion and murkiness that for almost a century has plagued the foundations of quantum mechanics, in spite of the theory's extraordinary usefulness and power. The second, less famous, problem has been with us at least as long: there seems to be nothing in physics that singles out 'the present moment'. Albert Einstein called this the problem of 'the Now'. Both problems are symptoms of the exclu-

sion from physical science of the perceiving subject, and are solved by restoring what the ancient Greeks removed. (2014)

Quantum Theory

In quantum theory the great paradox is the collapse of the wave function. As quoted in Appendix VIII, physicist Sean Carroll argues that there is no problem once the many-worlds theory is accepted. This is a perfectly valid argument for physical entities, but an inescapable consequence is that observers are all in the same physical world. But as explained in Chapter 27, confirmation of Wigner's friend shows us that conscious individuals live in different versions of physical reality. Thus quantum entanglement, i.e. decoherence, cannot be the whole answer.

Carroll's argument is perfectly valid for all physical observers. The key point is that the conscious individual is not the physical observer. It is the field of information it produces, the world hologram. The physical reality of the observer is the quasi-classical world, which works as Carroll describes. But the world of the world hologram is a superworld, a second-logical-type phenomenon. As we have seen, only this formulation satisfies the requirements of Wigner's friend. Observer and individual, body and mind, exist in different types of world, at different levels of logical type. They operate differently. Only the world of the mind fulfils all the requirements.

Relativity

In relativity the great paradoxes are the passage of time and the Now. There is no explanation of how or why there should be such phenomena. Weyl's statement, quoted in Chapter 9, clearly resolves the issues at a stroke. That which brings reality to life is the gaze of the experiencing consciousness, crawling up the worldline of the observer. It is necessarily a third-logical-type phenomenon. In this light the passage of time and the Now make perfect sense. This is the consciousness that passes along the worldline of each of us, as we all routinely experience day in day out.

This is the explanation of how it all actually works. This does not go down well in the physics of the modern world. The difficulty in the modern mood of physicalism is it means this consciousness has to be 'outside' of physical reality, in other words an emergent property of the universe itself. This is automatically rejected.

The Subject & The Perceiving

The perceiving subject is the *me*, the world hologram, the mind, experienced by the *I*, the universe consciousness. The subject is the world hologram. The perceiving is the consciousness.

As Mermin describes, the unrelated long-standing problems in the two pillars of the new physics are resolved by recognising the role of the perceiving subject and restoring it to central significance. In quantum theory, the measurement problem is resolved because the paradoxical collapse dynamics is a second-logical-type phenomenon, operating in the superworld, the physical reality of the mind. In relativity, the Now, the ever-moving present moment that cannot occur in physics, is the third-logical-type operation of the experiencing consciousness, the perceiving. The net result is the ongoing transtemporal experience of reality, the unfolding dynamics we know as reality of the real world happening, the holographic-universe movie of life.

XV

The Quantum Computer Brain

As described in Chapter 30, the word mind is here used to mean the world hologram, the record of the observations made. The rest of the mind, carrying out all the other operations of the brain, is here considered to be the operating system of the body. And on the inside view all that is indeterminate. Naturally, in each world in which you exist you have a real, physical, determinate brain, in which all the specific neural processes are going on, all specifically defined. But in the superworld your brain is the superposed sum of these brains, a class-of-brains-as-a-brain. The implications are remarkable.

Multiple Drafts

The multiple drafts concept of mind put forward by philosopher Daniel Dennett (1991) serves to introduce this idea very nicely. As we generally experience, there is a train of thought going on in the mind, the succession of more or less connected thoughts or ideas in a logical sequential flow. This is flow of the thought process that one is aware of in the sensorium. But Dennett holds that the mind is constantly producing *many* trains of thought, outside of conscious awareness. Each one is like a first draft, a possible beginning, a seed idea of the way a new train of thought could develop in conscious awareness. When one such draft is noticed, and the train of thought followed consciously, this becomes the content of awareness, meaning the train of thought one is actually aware of.

Dennett's concept fits very well with our knowledge of the structure of the brain. It works as a massively-parallel, distributed network, which means a huge amount of computation is taking place simultaneously. So his idea is exactly what one would expect in a system of this nature. There are many different drafts, possible trains of thought, any one of which may surface to conscious awareness.

When we apply this concept to the individual on the inside view, we get something highly remarkable. In your superworld you exist in every possible brain that instantiates your world hologram. Thus in your superworld, your brain is the superposition of them all. And this means that you have every possible version of the multiple drafts in this superbrain of yours.

This means that effectively your brain works like a quantum computer. Essentially, a quantum computer works by superposing every possible variation of a computation in memory, and then running the computation. Thus it carries out every possible variation of the computation simultaneously. Quantum computers are still in their infancy, but if you could load a whole database into memory, superposed, you would be able to search the whole thing in one cycle of the computer, in just a tiny fraction of a second, however large. Effectively, we have the same kind of capability because of the superworld. In the class-of-worlds-as-a-world, the brain is a class-of-brains-as-a-brain, and thus it operates as a quantum computer, processing an unlimited variety of trains of thought simultaneously.

This is not a physical phenomenon. It has been proposed that the ordinary physical brain works like a quantum computer, but this does not stack up. The eminent mathematical physicist and philosopher Roger Penrose has long been interested in the nature of the mind. In his book *The Emperor's New Mind* (1989) he suggests a possible mechanism for the physical brain to operate as a quantum computer. But Tegmark, in his paper *Importance of quantum decoherence in brain processes* (1999), has shown this is impossible because the required conditions cannot possibly be present in the neural network of the brain. The phenomenon described here, however, is something completely different. It is not an operational effect in the physical neural network of the brain, but a second-logical-type phenomenon – the superposition of all possible neural networks that instantiate this world hologram. It is purely a phenomenon that arises because the brain actually in use is a superposition of all the brains in the superworld. As Tegmark explains, one human brain cannot be a quantum computer. But a class-of-brains-as-a-brain cannot fail to be.

This explains why the creative process is not only incomprehensible but completely inscrutable. Where do creative ideas come from? Now we know. They are there already. All the ideas you could possibly have are present in your brain, at all times, just outside of conscious awareness. No wonder creativity is so utterly beyond our ordinary mortal ken. It also explains why the deep unconscious, beyond memory, is so completely impossible to understand, and even seems alien in a way. On the inside view it is indeterminate.

XVI

Relative Onticity

As described in Appendix XII each of the two quantum mechanical dynamics is causal on the other, alternately. This is a special case of what theoretical physicist Harald Atmanspacher calls relative onticity:

> The central point of the concept of relative onticity is that states and properties of a system, which belong to an epistemic description in a particular domain, can be considered as ontic from the perspective of another domain. (2005, 19)

(Epistemic, rather than ontic, means it is a matter of knowledge *about* the world, rather than the fundamental existence of the world.)

Unilateral Relative Onticity

On the outside view the record of observations that defines the inside view is defined by the physical form in which it is instantiated. The physical is ontic. On the inside view the determinacy of the instantiating physical reality is defined by the world hologram. In this physical frame of reference this information is ontic. As each observation is added to the world hologram, the definition of the metaworld is changed, thus the quantum-mechanical frame of reference of the relative state is redefined. Effectively, the wave function changes; the collapse dynamics operates.

Thus there are dual unilateral relative onticities: a dualism of ontologies. Each is ontic, alternately. The making of each observation happens because of the progression of the linear dynamics. Then, the effective change of the snapshot, and thus the linear dynamics, happens because of the observation made. There is an alternating, unilateral onticity.

The linear dynamics is fundamental within the context of a specific quasi-classical world, a specific physical 'snapshot' of the world as described in Chapter 28. Within this domain the progression of the linear dynamics alters the position of the subjective frame of reference, which passes along the worldline into the future. In due course this time evolution of the physical world causes the next observation to be made. The physical is ontic.

This brings about change of the quantum-mechanical frame of reference, the snapshot, in which the linear dynamics operates. Thus there is a new superworld with a new linear dynamics. The world hologram is ontic.

In this new version of the superworld the time evolution of the physical world continues. Thus the dynamics operate alternately as the standard formulation defines, as described in Appendix XII.

Triune

The vital moving viewpoint is of a third logical type, and thus the complete ontology is triune as described in Chapter 17. As illustrated in Figure 28.2, the viewpoint we know as the present moment, Einstein's Now, follows both linear and collapse dynamics alternately. Naturally, a phenomenon contextual to both types of dynamics is required. This moving viewpoint is able to move in two different ways, in different domains, *because* it is contextual to both, a third-logical-type phenomenon. This is how the two dynamics are actually enacted in the same system. That is how the cycle of the standard formulation actually operates, in the movement of the viewpoint of the third-logical-type consciousness, the 'projector'.

XVII

Inside-View Physics

The world is a real physical world, but it operates like a movie or a virtual reality. In other words, the fundamental structure of this domain is of course physical, exactly as defined in modern physics, but the time evolution of the world encountered is virtual. There is only the appearance of the passage of time, and only the appearance of the world changing. These are both purely subjective phenomena, produced by the moving Now. Thus the only operational dynamics are inside-view phenomena. These are essentially information processes. This is the physics of the superworld, inside-view physics.

Information As Primary

The idea of information as fundamental has a considerable history. As the eminent theoretical physicist John Wheeler stated:

> ... it is not unreasonable to imagine that information sits at the core of physics (1998, 340)

Tegmark has developed this idea in detail as he describes in his book *Our Mathematical Universe* (2014). In QBism, Fuchs simply says:

> Quantum states are not things–instead information. (2010)

This is exactly the nature of physical reality, but only on the inside view. On the inside view, the determinacy, the quantum state, is defined by the world hologram, a field of information.

As described in Appendix III, it is held in QBism that only the world defined by experience is real, but of course the objective physical reality is real also. There are two different types of world defined by the quantum theory when taken at face value. The full resolution is an ontological dualism as described in Appendix XVI.

As described in the text, the superworld is determinate only where defined by the world hologram, a field of information. This is why this information is the 'preferred basis' defining reality as described in Appendix IX. But this is not of course a causal process in the ordinary sense. The world hologram does not actually make the superworld the way it is, any more than redness causes a jar of marbles to have been filled with only red marbles in it. It is just that the marbles were selected on that basis. In just the same way, the superworld is a 'set-selection' phenomenon, meaning that the worlds in the class are 'selected' because they contain the world hologram, but the world hologram does not do the selecting. The world hologram, a field of information, is only *effectively* ontic.

The Virtual Passage of Time

As has been described, the passage of time is virtual. There is only the appearance of time passing, like the countryside from inside the train. Nothing happens in ordinary reality. As Weyl states, only to the gaze of consciousness does the world come to life, as it passes along the worldline. And this passage along the worldline is virtual also, of course. As described in Appendix XI this is the result of the experience of the wave function by consciousness. The effect is that the definition of the position in space-time is constantly changing, being redefined as further and further into the future, along the worldline. This is the quale of the experiencing of the wave function, meaning this is 'what it is like' to experience this transtemporal definition of the physical reality. As a result, in experience, the linear dynamics operates. The time evolution of the definition of the objective world progresses, as the wave function defines. In effect time passes.

The Virtual Happening of Events

The operation of the collapse dynamics is also virtual. Like the frames of a movie on a reel of celluloid film, the static objective physical reality just instantiates the sequence of physical states. Thus the sequence of states of the world hologram just exists, instantiated, permanently, in the sequence of snapshots, in objective physical reality, as symbolised in Figure XVII.

This is just like the sequence of moments in space-time in Figure 9, except that this is portraying a sequence of snapshots in the quantum concept of time, as described in Chapter 28. Each snapshot is a specific state of the holographic universe, defined by a specific state of the world hologram. As each observation is made, the moving viewpoint passes from snapshot to snapshot, creating the effect of the operation of my world hologram. Since this is what one experiences, and it takes a moving viewpoint to iterate the sequence of states of the world hologram, we know this is what is happening.

This sequence is experienced *as* the world changing, but, just as in the movies, only the picture changes. In a movie it is the sequence of frames. In the physical reality of the world hologram it is the sequence of physical frames of reference, each one a specific version of the holographic universe. Thus the operation of the physical reality en-

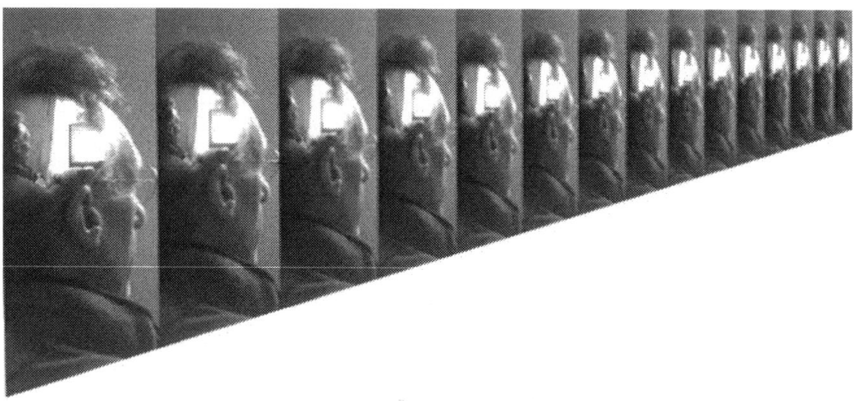

Figure XVII: A sequence of mind states in a sequence of snapshots.

countered is of the *logical type* of a movie, or a virtual reality, each frame being *made of* real physical world, snapshots. The sequence is experienced, as the viewpoint changes, moving along the sequence of snapshots. In other words, the happening of events is a virtual phenomenon, like the moving picture in the movies.

How Reality Actually Works

So the time evolutions of both dynamics, linear and collapse, are essentially virtual phenomena. This is why the operation of either of these phenomena is inexplicable on the outside view. They operate only on the inside view. The alternating progress of the two dynamics, described in Chapter 28, gives rise to the effect of transtemporal physical reality. The holographic-universe movie of life runs.

In our current scientific worldview it seems obvious that the viewpoint moves because the physical reality itself progresses. Things happen because all the atoms and molecules of the world move and interact; and as a result the frame of reference of the observer changes. Meanwhile, as a result, internally, the world hologram is changed, reflecting the changes in the outside world. That is the naturally assumed worldview, and the current paradigm. This is a perfectly correct description of the mechanics. This describes the algorithms of how reality actually works: how and why things happen as they do. But none of it actually happens except in the moving viewpoint.

Relativity defines the four-dimensional space-time, matter-and-energy block universe. Quantum theory defines the totality of all possible versions of such a universe, all possible snapshots, the many physical worlds. The two different kinds of time operate in these two domains. But they only operate because of the moving viewpoint. This is how reality actually works. The dynamics are mathematical functions, algorithms. The universe itself is static, but these algorithms are experienced in action as the moving viewpoint moves alternately in these two different domains. And the result is the operation of the cycle in the standard formulation. And thus the alternating cycle of the two different kinds of time effectively enacted, as described in Chapter 28.

The Great Thought

In the holographic universe information is not just centrally important but ontologically fundamental. As Jeans stated:

> The universe begins to look more like a great thought than a great machine. (1930, 187)

This is precisely the case on the inside view. The time evolution of physical reality is brought to life by the progression of states of the world hologram in the consciousness of the universe itself. This is an information process, the effective adding of each observation to the record of observations. This results in the time evolution of the holographic universe encountered. This is the realm of inside-view physics. Objective physical reality is the structure, but it is static. Nothing actually happens 'out there'. The transtemporal experience of the evolving holographic universe is inside-view physics in action.

Understanding the time evolution of the world as a virtual phenomenon, idiosyncratic to oneself, ratifies the extraordinary properties of the inside view. This in turn makes possible the reconnection with the whole of the operational identity, and that brings about transformation. As great minds in both philosophy and physics have noted, you are the world. As above so below. This is a participatory holographic universe. The empowering plugins for the standard psyche are described at the end of Chapter 31. The benefits would appear to be unlimited.

Acknowledgements

I am very grateful to Matthew Donald and Saibal Mitra for helpful comments and guidance with the physics. My heartfelt thanks go out to all my friends who helped me bring this work to fruition, particularly David Orr, Neil Wilkinson, Stephen King, David Robson, Lyn Goswell, Arabella Tresilian, Matthew Hemson, Alex Stansfield and Bob Tyrrell. I am also very grateful to Rachel Beckett for editing the manuscript and making numerous helpful suggestions.

Glossary

Words in the lexicon of the new paradigm, meaning new terms presented here or used in a manner specific to this context, are in italics.

Andromeda paradox: Given relativity, simply changing the direction in which you are walking alters whether distant events happened some time ago, or have yet to happen. So, either you are changing the physical state of affairs in the Andromeda galaxy, which physics does not allow, or you are simply changing what is true for you. The latter must mean that objectively both versions of the world are true all the time: i.e. the universe is a block universe. It is all 'there'. This is the Rietdijk-Putnam-Penrose argument in a nutshell. This is all addressed in depth by Savitt (2017). (The counter-position is a changing 3D world, and the debate gets quite heated. However, as described in the text, both paradigms are true. While 'actually', objectively, the world is static 4D block universe, 'effectively', subjectively, meaning in the moving viewpoint of consciousness, it is a changing 3D world.)

Anthropomorphism: The attribution of human traits, such as personality, to non-human entities. It is considered to be an innate tendency in humans.

Applied epistemology: "Applied epistemology in general is the study of whether systems of investigation that purport to be seeking the truth are well engineered to lead to true beliefs about the world. Theorists of knowledge, as epistemologists are sometimes known, routinely examine truth-seeking practices like science and mathematics to find out whether they are capable of delivering the goods they seek." (Laudan, 2006).

Archetype: An original or fundamental pattern, of which all things of the same type are representations or copies. Also used to refer to collective representations or primordial thoughts arising across the boundaries of cultures, traditions and ideologies.

Attractor: Any state toward which a system tends to gravitate.

Attractor: Strange: An attractor in a complex system. Rather than a specific state, the system gravitates toward certain tendencies, or behaviours.

Avatar: In computer games this means the digital representation of a person in the game. Here the word is used for the representation of a person in the world hologram. Just as the world hologram is the integrated synthesis of all observations made of the world, an avatar is the integrated synthesis of all observations made of that person. The avatar of oneself at the centre of the world hologram is the integrated synthesis of all observations made of one-self: the self-avatar figure.

Bayesian probability: A method of working of out the probabilities of what is likely to happen in the world, based on what has been observed in the past and the implications of this information.

Block universe: This means that all existence in time is equally real. The world is 'there' in the future just as it is 'there' in the distance in space. A useful article is presented by physicist Paul Davies (2006a)

Body Schema: The mental image of the body, especially in relation to spa-tial awareness and movement. It is a postural model that keeps track of the body's spatial properties, such as limb position and the shape of the body surface.

Born rule: This is the law of quantum mechanics that gives the probability of a specific result in a quantum-mechanical experiment.

Catch 22: A circular double bind: no work available unless you have exper-ience, to get which you need to work.

Category error: This is a mistake of logic in which something that belonging to a particular category is treated as if it belongs to a different category.

Class-of-worlds-as-a-world: A descriptive technical term for the super-world.

Collapse dynamics: The abrupt apparent change of the wave function on observation. The wave function in quantum mechanics is defined by the Schrödinger wave equation, according to which the system evolves, on ad-vancing the time parameter, into a linear superposition of different states. This is the linear dynamics. But actual measurements always find the physical system in a definite state, hence a secondary 'collapse' dynamics is somehow enacted, giving rise to a specific actualised property of a subatomic particle, e.g. a specific value for position or momentum. The inability to observe this process directly has given rise to different interpretations of quantum mechanics, and poses a key set of questions that each interpretation must answer. Here this phenomenon is shown to operate at a different level of logical type to the linear dynamics. This authenticates both Everett and QBism.

Correlation: Correlated things have properties that alter 'together' meaning in sync, like power cuts and conceptions. They are statistically related to each other i.e. co-related. Quantum correlation means that each of two systems has information about the other. This leads to co-relation of the probabilities of events in the future. (This is closely related to quantum entanglement which means there is no separate physical definition of either system.)

Consciousness: The word consciousness is used for two very different classes of phenomena, named by Chalmers psychological consciousness and phenomenal consciousness. Ned Block calls the first 'access consciousness', which he defines as the answer to the question: "What makes neuronal representations available for thought, decision, reporting and action?" (2003, 8). This is sapience, meaning the intellectual information processing capability. This is the system that produces the virtual-reality representation of the world that *gets* experienced, the *contents* of consciousness. The world hologram is the cumulative result. The experiencing consciousness is called phenomenal consciousness by both Block and Chalmers. This is the sentience, the capacity to experience, though this may not be precisely the meaning defined by Block who first coined the term. Here phenomenal consciousness is taken to be necessarily a property of the entire system, universe consciousness. Chalmers stops short of making this kind of equivalence, but Bitbol adopts it wholeheartedly, referring to it as Mind.

Copenhagen interpretation: This was the first general attempt to understand the world defined by quantum mechanics. Essentially, since all physical systems are made of quanta, which generally do not have definite properties prior to being observed, the system is in the same state i.e. the state of the system is indeterminate. Only when observed does it acquire one specific state or another. This feature is known as wavefunction collapse.

Decoherence: The process whereby the quantum-mechanical state of any macroscopic system is rapidly correlated with that of its environment. This process typically makes all the attributes of the system determinate. However, this does not properly account for wavefunction collapse.

Destiny: The predetermined future. The inevitable course of events: given it is noon, it will be midnight in twelve hours. Also a person's fate.

Destiny: Interactive: The alteration of the destiny in the physical reality of this individual's superworld. As observations are made, the Bayesian probabilities of the future in this physical frame of reference are altered. This never alters the destiny of objective physical reality, only the version of physical reality this individual will likely experience in the future.

Determinate: Precisely determined or limited or defined, actually so. In quantum terms, a property having only one specific value.

Dynamics: The way the system changes in time mechanically, e.g. the way the motion of an object alters under the action of a force. In quantum theory the dynamics of the system is defined in two different ways, resulting in the measurement problem. See also Collapse dynamics, Linear dynamics.

Egoism: Egoism here means the belief that acting in one's own best interests is the only criterion that matters.

Emergent: Emergence is when a system as a whole has properties that its parts do not have on their own. Transport is an emergent property of a properly assembled vehicle.

Empirical: Coming from the direct evidence of experiment. Not just theoretical.

Entropy: This is a measurable physical property of a system. Essentially this is the amount of information that is needed to fully specify the state of the system.

Epistemic: Relating to knowledge about the world.

Event: Interaction of matter and energy at a specific point in the four-dimensional space-time matrix.

Frame of reference: The basic frame of reference is a coordinate system i.e. one which uses numbers to uniquely determine the position of a place, or object in space – the numbers are the 'coordinates': for instance distance from a specific point of origin on a journey.

Function: A mathematical function defines a relationship between two things, the input and the output. So a function called distance_travelled, would take the speed and the elapsed time travelling, as two inputs, and multiply them to give the distance travelled, the output. The distance travelled is a *function of* the speed and the time taken. The function takes the inputs and returns the output.

Function: Wave: In physics, a mathematical function that returns the likelihood of a possible state of a physical system, e.g. the position or momentum of a subatomic particle. For any given possible event at a given elapsed time, the wave function returns the probability of that event.

Functional identity: This is the identity of the entity that actually operates in reality. This is defined by the record of observations including all the active data and algorithms in the personal psychology that embody the capacity to form thoughts and feelings, make decisions and determine action.

Hilbert space: A mathematical space with an infinite number of dimensions. This is a mathematical way of defining objects of many dimensions, using the mathematical techniques used for ordinary three-dimensional objects and spaces. In quantum mechanics this is the state space in which the state vector defines the quantum state of a physical entity or system.

Higher self: The full identity of the conscious individual.

Holographic universe, *see* Universe: Holographic.

Indeterminate: Not accurately determined. In quantum terms, not accurately determined, *or even determinable*: 'physically uncertain', meaning a property having multiple values for what is actually so.

Intersection: An intersection is a group of items that belong to two different sets. So an intersection of two roads is the group of points in space that belongs to both roads.

Intersection of worlds: The intersection of worlds is the group of correlated events recorded in the world hologram.

Individual: The entity defined by the world hologram, defined in Everett's formulation as the record of observations. This is literally, ontologically, undividable: it is a holographic structure of information, and holograms cannot be divided. If you take half of a hologram away you do not get two different parts defined by different information. Instead you get two holograms, defined by the same information as the original, but with half the detail, half the resolution. See also Observer.

Inside view: The frame of reference of a conscious individual. In Tegmark's terms, the view of the world of a self-aware substructure in it.

Interactive Destiny: see Destiny: Interactive.

Karma: The idea that actions and even intentions of an individual influence the future of that individual. Thus the making of destiny or fate from personal cause. In practical terms, the kinds of things you do to others are also likely to be the kinds of things that others do to you; what goes around comes around. Here karma is explained as the increasing tendency of strange attractors to reproduce the types of significant actions observed.

Law of attraction: The idea that like attracts like, so that if you think about the things you want they will be drawn to you, even if these outcomes are completely outside of your ability to influence in any ordinary way. The same concept is traditionally known as sympathetic magic.

Lexicon: The special language, or stock of terms, of a particular paradigm. The language of biology deals with structures of living organisms: phylum and oedema are part of the lexicon. The lexicon of logical types as ontologically fundamental, for instance, provides the language-components superworld and class-of-worlds-as-a-world.

Life-line: The term used by Weyl to refer to the worldline of the person.

Linear dynamics: The time evolution of a quantum system as defined by the quantum wave function, according to which the system evolves, on advancing the time parameter, into a linear superposition of different states. On observation, it seems, the multiple superposed states of the system 'collapse' into a specific determinate actuality. This is the collapse dynamics.

Logical type: The vital distinction between a set or class of elements and a single one of those elements, first denoted by Bertrand Russell. The latter is termed first or primitive logical type and the former second logical type.

Macroscopic: Large enough to be perceived by the unaided eye.

Many-minds theory: The many-worlds theory shows that all possibilities become real, and the observer is in a state of superposition following the making an observation. Since we know from direct experience that only one version of events is experienced, it must follow that there are different versions of the mind of the observer, one for each possible version of the observation made. Only the world of the mind, therefore, defines a determinate state.

Many-Worlds theory: The common name for a class of theory first proposed by Hugh Everett's in 1957. This demonstrates resolution of the measurement problem in quantum theory: Everett shows that there is no need to postulate a physical collapse dynamics – hence the existence of all possible worlds – since there is the *appearance* of collapse from the relative perspective of each specific individual.

Measurement problem: The wave function evolves according to the quantum wave equation into a linear superposition of different states, but actual measurements always find the physical system in a definite state. By definition no one system can perform both of these operations simultaneously, but this is what is required in order to explain what is observed in experiment.

Mind: Usually described as the faculties of cognition, e.g. consciousness, perception, thinking, judgement, imagination, and memory. Here the word mind is used for a *subset* of these facilities, the memory only, meaning the record of observations, the world hologram. The rest of the information processing faculty is taken to be an attribute of the physical observer, the operating system of the body. This gives rise to the world hologram, but on the inside view it is all indeterminate except where observed, and thus defined by the world hologram.

Mind: unconscious see Unconscious.

Moving viewpoint: see Viewpoint, moving.

Moravec jump: The transition to a new life-line, on a different worldline, on the making of the first observation in the different version of the world.

Multi-solipsism: QBism holds that only what is experienced (here referred to as what is observed) is determinate. Thus all else, including others in the world, are defined solely where observed by this person. Since in this person's physical reality only this person is real, this is a form of solipsism. At the same time, all individuals, each with their own physical reality, are acknowledged as existing and real on their own terms, hence multi-solipsism.

Multiverse: Another name for the universe of all possible worlds.

Neural Network: The interconnected network of neurons in the brain, numbering around 100 billion. This is the physical structure of the biological computer that carries out all our mental processes such as perception, reasoning, and judgement.

Observation problem: The unresolved problem of how (or if) wave function collapse occurs. The wave function evolves according to the quantum wave equation into a linear superposition of different states, but actual measurements always find the physical system in a definite state. This appears to mean that the observation 'did something' to the process under examination. Although many kinds of observation do have an effect on what is observed, this collapse of the states definitely happens when no cause can be attributed to the making of the observation. Unobserved, reality is quantum, taking all possible forms, but in reality, i.e. observed, reality is classical always taking a specific form. And so the observation problem is the problem of how the classical world emerges from the quantum world. Decoherence goes a long way toward resolving this issue.

Observer: The physical entity that uses sensory apparatus to produce a representation of its environment which is recorded in memory. It gives rise to the individual, the person on the inside view. In classical science the term person can be synonymous with the term observer: physically we are body-minds, to which classical physics applies. However, as described by Everett, we know from quantum physics that following the making of an observation, the physical body-mind holds multiple versions of the inside view, here the world hologram, superposed: the quantum-mechanical dynamics applies only to the individual.

Observer-dependent: see Reality: Observer-Dependent:

Ontic: Ontological, of the fundamental nature of being.

Onticity: Relative: The physical reality, the actuality, is relative to the viewpoint, the frame of reference in physics.

Ontology: A conceptualisation of the nature of being, or the kinds of things that have fundamental existence.

Ontologically fundamental: This is used here to mean on a par with physical existence as primal and fundamental.

Operating system: In a computer this is the system software that manages the hardware and provides the context in which information processes operate, and the facilities they require to function.

Paradigm: A philosophical or theoretical framework. In science the paradigm includes not only the set of familiar concepts in the field, the theories and ideas in use, but also the standards for what constitutes legitimate contributions in that field. In this sense the term was coined by Kuhn.

Person: The conscious subject of experience that engages with the physical reality encountered. A psychic entity, defined by a specific world hologram, referred to here interchangeably as the individual.

Phenomenal consciousness: See Consciousness.

Protagonist: The main character, used here to mean the entity to which the dynamics of physics are real phenomena.

Psyche: The functional identity as an operational entity.

Psychological consciousness: See Consciousness.

QBism: A modern update of Quantum Bayesianism.

Qualia: The purely subjective phenomena of experience. The properties of experience that have no correlate in physical reality.

Quantum: The minimum amount of any physical entity involved in an interaction.

Quantum Bayesianism: A view of quantum theory that applies Bayesian probability to quantum mechanics, principally developed by Caves, Fuchs, Schack and Mermin.

Quantum gravity: This is the physics that unifies gravity with the other three fundamental forces.

Quantum jump: The spontaneous change in the quantum state: the exercise of the collapse dynamics.

Quantum karma: Karma as a result of confirmation bias due to unconscious expectations.

Quantum mechanics: The mathematical formulation of quantum theory, defining how a quantum, or a quantum system, moves and interacts.

Quantum state: The state in which a physical system exists. This is usually described by a wave function. As this is a probabilistic definition this defines the likelihood of all possible events involving this system.

Quantum theory: A branch of physics providing a mathematical description of the dynamics of the fundamental physical reality: the way matter and energy interact, at the subatomic quantum level, and the relative likelihood of such events. In classical or Newtonian mechanics, the probabilities of events are definite and specific, but unknown for most kinds of events most of the time. In the new physics of quantum theory the definitions of physical systems and events are inherently probabilistic.

Reality: Observer-Dependent: The physical reality determinate where observed by this observer i.e. dependent on the observer for definition.

Reality: Perceptual: The reality as experienced by the individual in the sensorium, and recorded in memory, the whole forming the world hologram.

Reality: Physical: That which is determinately real in a given frame of reference. On the outside view this is the quasi-classical world. On the inside view this is the class-of-worlds-as-a-world.

Reality: Quantum: The physical reality defined by the quantum state. In the ordinary world this is indeterminate only at very small scales and for very short periods of time. In the World this is indeterminate except where observed.

Record of observations: Record of all observations made of the environment, and of the self. This is the state of the memory in Everett's many-worlds theory. The world hologram is the integrated synthesis of the record of observations. The record of observations of the self forms the self-avatar figure at the centre of the world hologram.

Religion: Religion here means not just our relation to the sacred and the spiritual but actual reconnection to the divinity of nature, as in religare.

Retrodict: This is when a new discovery or a new perspective explains something known from history that previously had no explanation. Retrospectively, it is clear that this is the reason for the phenomenon.

Rietdijk-Putnam-Penrose argument: Essentially this holds that the Andromeda paradox means the universe is a block universe, with full mathematical demonstration. This is addressed in depth by Savitt (2017).

Right Action: Doing no harm. Closely akin to the Do Not's of the Ten Commandments.

Sapience: The intellectual information processing capability. The system that processes information, and produces understanding and insight.

Schrödinger wave equation: The fundamental equation for describing and predicting quantum-mechanical behaviour.

Schrödinger's cat: A thought experiment by Erwin Schrödinger to illustrate the absurdity of quantum theory.

Self-concept: The mental image one has of oneself, the complete concept one has built up of who and what one is.

Self-avatar: The self-identity figure at the centre of the world hologram: the holographic field of information defining the determinacy of the body on the inside view.

Sensorium: The sensory apparatus, the faculties of an organism's perception considered as a whole. The world hologram is the experiential attribute of the sensorium.

Sentience: The experiencing capability, the phenomenal consciousness.

Snapshot: This here refers to the quantum state of the world, the state of the whole system at a particular point in time. The term is coined by Deutsch in his explanation of the quantum concept of time.

Stochastic: Randomly determined.

Soul: Traditional name for the world hologram experienced by consciousness, the mind as defined by the record of observations. This is the real person 'in here', meaning the field of information that if uploaded into a new body would be the same person in all functional terms.

Solipsism: The philosophical idea that the self is the only existing reality, and that all other reality, including the external world and other persons, are representations in the mind of this individual, having no independent existence.

Superstring: This is a way of modelling the physical components of nature in terms of frequencies at the very smallest scale.

Superposition Principle: This principle holds that the net result of a phenomenon at a given place and time caused by two or more casual processes is the sum of the results which would have been caused by each causal process individually. The quantum superposition of physical phenomena is simply this principle applied to the results of applying multiple wave functions to a single physical context: in other words, adding together the wave functions of two or more quantum states gives the net physical reality.

Superworld: The effective physical environment defined by the superposition of all worlds containing the world hologram. The result is the effect of the holographic universe. This provides the ontology for a QBism type of world, determinate solely where observed. Vaidman calls this kind of world a relative or perspectival world, and he also states that this kind of world is considered basic in some approaches. This is the physical reality of an individual on the inside view in Tegmark's classification: as defined by the record of observations. This is Everett's relative state.

Terror management: The concept that psychological dissonance arises from the fundamental instinct for self-preservation faced with the inevitability of death. The conflict produces a natural terror. This is then managed by displacement activities such as keeping busy, or belief in immortality.

Time: In common usage this refers to the linear dimension of space-time, in which durations of events and the intervals between them can be measured and compared, and along which events may be sequenced. In general use, a measuring system used to sequence and compare events, their duration and so on. See also Time: Quantum.

Time: Quantum: Whereas the concept of time in classical and relativistic physics is based on sequence of moments in space-time, the quantum concept of time is based on the sequence of quantum states defining a physical system. As stated by Lockwood this is a dimension running, so to speak, perpendicular to time and space.

Time evolution: The time evolution of a system is the change of the state of the system, as the viewpoint progresses along the time dimension. In the mathematics of physics this simply means advancing the time parameter of the relevant equation, usually denoted as *t*. In Newtonian mechanics, mechanics, the time evolution of the physical state of the system is the change in the configuration of the matter and energy in space-time, as the time parameter is increased. In the linear dynamics of quantum mechanics, the same thing is defined, within the context of a system with a specific quantum state, but the definition becomes increasingly indeterminate over time. Time evolution in the collapse dynamics is the change of the quantum state defining this frame of reference, as described in Chapter 28. This is the enactment of the quantum concept of time.

Transtemporal: Literally, transcending time. The word is used here in the sense applied in philosophical literature to mean enduring through time, an entity or phenomenon genuinely passing through time.

Trim tab: This is a meta-control that biases the steering. On large ships this is a small extra rudder at the end of the rudder. By moving the rudder, the trim tab has a disproportionate effect on the direction of the ship.

Triune: Three in one. A trinity in unity.

Unconscious, the: The conscious awareness is the immediate perception. The rest of the psychological domain is the unconscious. Jung differentiates between two attributes of the unconscious, personal and collective.

Unconscious: Personal: The personal unconscious is defined by Jung as those attributes of the mind, once conscious, that are accessible but not in immediate conscious awareness. With the immediate perception included, this is world hologram as a whole.

Unconscious: Collective: As Jung describes, the rest of the psychological system that is not part of the conscious awareness, and not part of the personal unconscious, is the collective unconscious. This is an attribute of the operating system of the body that is common to all members of the species. As he states it consists primarily of archetypes. But these fields of information are not static but dynamic, and "... give definite form to certain psychic contents." (1969, 43). It thus exists across the boundaries of individuals' identities in a dynamic manner, thus providing a rationale for the remarkable type of properties he describes. This accounts for the mysterious zeitgeist of human cultures. This also explains how a population can be manipulated politically when powerful archetypes are energised through the media.

Universe: Everything that exists. Originally this meant simply everything in space and time. Now it has come to mean the space of all possible worlds, all existing in space-time. That used to be called the multiverse.

Universe consciousness: The awareness of all conscious entities. This is to the moments of reality experienced as the movie projector is to the frames of the movie film. It is a ubiquitous transcendental phenomenon. It is referred to in many cultures as spirit.

Universe: Holographic: The world as defined by quantum gravity. This shows that the three-dimensional world is completely defined on the two-dimensional boundary at the outer edge. This is the effect of the superworld. The observed surface is the only determinacy.

Vedas: A large body of religious texts from ancient India. Vedic science is the natural science of the Vedas, e.g. Ayur Veda, the science of healing.

Viewpoint: The frame of reference of a specific perspective.

Viewpoint: Moving. The moving viewpoint is the gaze of consciousness in Weyl's statement quoted on page 32.

Wave function: See Function: Wave.

Wigner's Friend: This is a thought experiment, very similar to Schrödinger's cat, in which not only the result of the experiment but also the experimenter is found to be in an indeterminate state.

World: The objective physical environment. This is well defined by Vaidman: "A world is the totality of (macroscopic) objects: stars, cities, people, grains of sand, etc. in a definite classically described state." (2002). A physical reality on the outside view in Tegmark's classification.

World: Meta see superworld.

World: Quasi-classical. Classical means it is a world of Newtonian mechanics, and essentially all real and there, just as we imagine it to be. It is quasi-classical because it only appears to be a Newtonian world, but is not like that at all at very small scales of reality where everything is defined solely by quantum probabilities. So a quasi-classical world operates exactly like an ordinary, Newtonian, classical-physics world in everyday life, but do quantum mechanical experiments on it and it turns out it is all indeterminate 'underneath'.

World hologram: The holographic field of information representing the entire record of observations. It is experienced subjectively as the perceptual reality of the individual. This is an internally generated virtual reality, representing the physical environment. This is mentally projected onto the environment to match up with the physical reality known to the individual by these observations. This is the display of the navigation equipment of the individual. Because it coincides perfectly with the details of the environment, a basic attribute of the functionality, it is experienced *as* the spatially distributed environment in which the individual exists. Thus it is usually not appreciated that what one is actually experiencing is 'in here' as opposed to 'out there'. The self-avatar figure is the central component.

Worldline: The path of an object in four-dimensional space-time, tracing its location in space at each moment in time: a central concept in modern physics.

References

Adams, D.: 1979, *The Hitchhiker's Guide to the Galaxy*, Pan Books, London.

Albert, D. & Loewer, B.: 1988, "Interpreting the Many Worlds Interpretation", *Synthese*, 77, 195-213.

Atmanspacher, H. & Primas, H.: 2005, "Epistemic and Ontic Quantum Realities ", <http://philsci-archive.pitt.edu/938/1/cfvw.pdf>.

Bacciagaluppi, Guido.: 2012 "The Role of Decoherence in Quantum Mechanics", *The Stanford Encyclopedia of Philosophy* (*Summer 2012 Edition*), Edward N. Zalta (ed.), <https://plato.stanford.edu/archives/sum2012/entries/qm-decoherence/>

Barbour, J.: 1999, *The End of Time*, Weidenfeld & Nicolson, London.

Barrett, J.: 1999, *The Quantum Mechanics of Minds and Worlds*, Oxford University Press.

Barrett, J.: 2008, "Everett's Relative-State Formulation of Quantum Mechanics", *The Stanford Encyclopedia of Philosophy*, Zalta, E. (ed.), <http://stanford.library.sydney.edu.au/archives/fall2008/entries/qm-everett/>.

Barrett, J.: 2011, "Research Interests", <http://www.lps.uci.edu/lps_bios/jabarret>.

Bekenstein, J.: 2003, "Information in the holographic universe", *Scientific American*, 289(2): 58-65.

Bitbol, M.: 1990, "Perspectival Realism and Quantum Mechanics", P. Lahti & P. Mittelstaedt, Symposium on the foundations of modern physics 1990, <philsci-archive.pitt.edu/1957/>.

Bitbol, M.: 2008, "Is Consciousness primary?", <philsci-archive.pitt.edu/4007/>.

Block, N.: 1995, "On a confusion about a function of consciousness", *Beha-*

vioural and Brain Sciences, 18: Pages 227-47, Cambridge.

Carnap, R., 1963. "Carnap's Intellectual Biography", *The Philosophy of Rudolf Carnap*, P. A. Schilpp (ed.), pp. 3–84. Open Court, La Salle, Illinois.

Carroll, S.: 2019, "Splitting the Universe", *Aeon*, Weintraub, P. (ed), <https://aeon.co/essays/how-the-many-worlds-theory-of-hugh-everett-s-plit-the-universe>.

Chadwick, H.: 2008, *The Confessions*, Oxford University Press.

Chalmers, D.: 1995, "Facing Up to the Problem of Consciousness", *Journal of Consciousness Studies* 2(3):200-19, <consc.net/papers/facing.html>.

Chalmers, D.: 1996, *The Conscious Mind*, Oxford University Press.

Changizi, M.: 2009, "The Value Of Being Aloof: Or, How Not To Get Absorbed In Someone Else's Abdomen", <www.science20.com/mark_changizi/value_being_aloof_or_how_not_get_absorbed_someone_else's_abdomen>.

Chown, M.: 2001, "Taming The Multiverse", *New Scientist*, Issue 2299.

Chown, M.: 2002, *The Universe Next Door*, Oxford University Press.

Constandi, M.: 2011, "Memory Contaminates Perception", *The Guardian*, <https://www.theguardian.com/science/neurophilosophy/2011/aug/17/memory-contaminates-perception>.

Cox, B., Ince, R. & Feachem, A.: 2017, The Infinite Monkey Cage – How to Build a Universe, William Collins, London.

Darwin, C.: 1981, *The Descent of Man and Selection in Relation To Sex*, Princeton Press.

Davies, P.: 2006a, "That Mysterious Flow", *Scientific American*, September, <https://www.scientificamerican.com/article/that-mysterious-flow-2006-02/>.

Davies, P.: 2006b, *The Goldilocks Enigma*, Allen Lane, London.

Dawkins, R.: 1998, *Unweaving the Rainbow*, Houghton Mifflin, Boston.

Dawkins, R.: 2016, *The God Delusion: 10th Anniversary Edition Paperback*, Penguin Random House.

Dennett, D.: 1988, "Quining Qualia", in Marcel, A. & Bisiach, E., eds, *Consciousness in Modern Science*, Oxford University Press.

Dennett, D.: 1991, *Consciousness Explained*, Little, Brown and Co., London.

Deutsch, D.: 1996, "Comment on "'Many Minds' Interpretations of Quantum Mechanics by Michael Lockwood"", *British Journal for the Philosophy of Science*, 47: 159 – 188.

Deutsch, D.: 1997, *The Fabric of Reality*, Allen Lane, London.

Deutsch, D.: 2011, *The Beginning of Infinity*, Viking Books, New York.

DeWitt, B.: 1970, "Quantum Mechanics and Reality", *Physics Today*, 23: 30–35.

Dijkgraaf, R.: 2019, "Einstein's Quantum Riddle", PBS, US.

Donald, M.: 1997, "On Many-Minds Interpretations Of Quantum Theory", <http://arxiv.org/abs/quant-ph/9703008>.

Donald, M.: 1998, A Many-Minds Interpretation Of Quantum Theory, <http://people.bss.phy.cam.ac.uk/~mjd1014/>.

Everett, H.: 1957, "'Relative State' Formulation of Quantum Mechanics", *Reviews of Modern Physics* 29: 454-462.

Everett, H.: 1973, "The Theory of the Universal Wave Function", *The Many-Worlds Interpretation of Quantum Mechanics*, DeWitt, B. & Graham, N. (eds.), pp 3-140, Princeton University Press, Princeton.

Fodor, J. 1992 "The big idea: Can there be a science of mind?" *Times Literary Supplement*, July 3: 5-7.

Friedman, T.: 2008, *Hot, flat, and crowded*, Farrar, Straus and Giroux, New York.

Friedman, T.: 2016, *Thank You for Being Late: An Optimist's Guide to Thriving in the Age of Accelerations*, Farrar, Straus and Giroux, New York.

Fuchs, C.: 2010, "QBism, the Perimeter of Quantum Bayesianism", <arxiv.org/abs/1003.5209v1>.

Fuchs, C., Mermin, N, & Schack, R.: 2013, "An Introduction to QBism with an Application to the Locality of Quantum Mechanics", <arxiv.org/abs/1311.5253>.

Gross, D.: 2005, "Concluding remarks", *23rd Solvay Conference*, Brussels.

Goldstein, R.: 2005, *Incompleteness: The Proof and Paradox of Kurt Godel*, Norton, New York.

Greene, B.: 1999, *The Elegant Universe*, Norton, New York.

Gribbin, J.: 1984, *In Search of Schrödinger's Cat*, Bantam Books, New York.

Hawking, S.: 1988, *A Brief History of Time*, Bantam Books, New York.

Hawking, S.: 2010, *The Grand Design*, Bantam Books, New York.

Heisenberg, W.: 1962, *Physics and Philosophy*, Allen & Unwin, London.

Herbert, N.: 1985, *Quantum Reality*, Anchor Books, New York.

Jeans, J.: 1930, *The Mysterious Universe*, The Cambridge University Press.

Jung, C.: 1933, *Modern Man in Search of a Soul*, Kegan Paul, Trench, Trubner and Co, London.

Jung, C.: 1963, *Memories, Dreams, Reflections*, Pantheon Books, New York.

Jung, C.: 1969, *The Archetypes and the Collective Unconscious*, Princeton University Press.

Kang, M. Hong, S. Blake, R. & Woodman, G.: 2011, "Visual working memory contaminates perception", *Psychonomic Bulletin Review*, <https://www.ncbi.nlm.nih.gov/pubmed/21713369>.

King, A.: 2006, *Let the Cat Turn Round: One Man's Traverse of the Twentieth Century*, CPTM, extract available at: <www.clubofrome.at/archive/the_club_of_rome_king.pdf>.

Kuhn, T.: 1962, *The Structure of Scientific Revolutions*, University of Chicago Press.

Laudan, L.: 2006, *Truth, Error, and Criminal Law, An Essay in Legal Epistemology*, Cambridge University Press.

Lockwood, M.: 1989, *Mind, Brain and the Quantum*, Blackwell, Oxford.

Lockwood, M.: 1996, "'Many Minds' Interpretations of Quantum Mechanics", *Brit. J. Phil. Sci.* 47: 159 – 188.

Lockwood, M.: 2005, *The Labyrinth of Time*, Oxford University Press, New York.

Lutyens, M.: 1983, *The Years of Fulfilment*, Avon Books, New York.

Meijer, D.: 2015, "The Universe as a Cyclic Organized Information System: John Wheeler's World Revisited", *NeuroQuantology*, **13**, Issue 1

Mermin, D.: 1989, "What's Wrong with this Pillow?", *Physics Today*, **42**, 4.

Mermin, D.: 2014, "Physics: QBism puts the scientist back into science", *Nature*, **507**, No. 7493, pp. 421-423.

Mitra, S.: 2009, "Changing the past by forgetting?", <http://arxiv.org/abs/0902.3825v1>.

Moore, W.: 1989, *Schrödinger: Life And Thought*, Cambridge University Press, pp 170-3.

Moravec, H.: 1998, "Simulation, Consciousness, Existence", <www.-frc.ri.cmu.edu/~hpm/project.archive/general.articles/1998/SimConEx.98.html>.

Musser, G.: 2002, "A Hole at the Heart of Physics", *Scientific American Magazine*, New York.

Murray, W.: 1951, *The Scottish Himalayan Expedition*, J.M. Dent & Sons Ltd., London.

Myrvold, W.: 2016, "Philosophical Issues in Quantum Theory", *The Stanford Encyclopedia of Philosophy* (Spring 2017 Edition), Zalta, E. (ed.), <http://stanford.library.sydney.edu.au/entries/qt-issues/>.

Nagel, Thomas, 1974, "What's it Like to be a Bat?", *The Philosophical Review*, 83(4): 435–450.

Pagels, H.: 1983, *The Cosmic Code*, Bantam Books, New York.

Penrose, R.: 1989, *The Emperor's New Mind*, Oxford University Press.

Petersen, A.: 1963 "The philosophy of Niels Bohr", *Bulletin of the Atomic Scientists*, **19**, 7.

Planck, M.: 1931, As quoted in *The Observer*, 25 January, p.17, column 3.

Planck, M.: 1949, *Wissenschaftliche Selbstbiographie. Mit einem Bildnis und der von Max von Laue gehaltenen Traueransprache*, Johann Ambrosius Barth Verlag, Leipzig, p. 22, as translated in *Scientific Autobiography and Other Papers*, trans. F. Gaynor, New York, pp. 33-34.

Poltorak, A.: 2019, "Wigner's Friend Paradox", <https://blogs.timesofisrael.com/wigners-friend-paradox/>.

Proietti, M., Pickston, A., Graffitti, F., Barrow, P., Kundys, D., Branciard, C., Ringbauer, M. & Fedrizzi, A.: 2019, "Experimental rejection of observer-independence in the quantum world", <https://arxiv.org/abs/1902.05080v2>.

Rovelli, C.: 1997, "Relational Quantum Mechanics", *International Journal of Theoretical Physics*, 35 (1996) pp. 1637-78.

Russell, B.: 1908, "Mathematical Logic as Based on the Theory of Types," *American Journal of Mathematics*, 30, 222-262, Appendix B.

Ryle, G.: 1949, *The Concept of Mind*, University of Chicago Press.

Saunders, S.: 2004, "What is probability?", *Quo Vadis Quantum Mechanics*, (eds.) Elitzur A., Dolev, S., & Kolenda, N., Springer-Verlag

Savitt, S.: 2017, "Being and Becoming in Modern Physics", *The Stanford Encyclopedia of Philosophy* (Fall 2017 Edition), Zalta, E. (ed.), <https://plato.stanford.edu/archives/fall2017/entries/spacetime-bebecome>.

Scholz, E.: 2004, "Philosophy as a cultural resource and medium of reflection for Hermann Weyl", <http://arxiv.org/abs/math/0409596>.

Schrödinger, E.: 1931, As quoted in *The Observer*, 11 January.

Smolin, L.: 2000, *Three Roads To Quantum Gravity*, Weidenfeld & Nicolson, London.

Speth, G.: 2013, "Shared Planet: Religion and Nature", BBC Radio 4 (1 October), <https://www.bbc.co.uk/sounds/play/b03bqws7>.

Spong, J.: 1998, *Why Christianity Must Change or Die*, Harper Collins, New York.

t'Hooft, G.: 1993, "Dimensional Reduction in Quantum Gravity", <http://arxiv.org/abs/gr-qc/9310026v2>.

Tegmark, M.: 1997, "The Interpretation of Quantum Mechanics: Many Worlds or Many Words?", <http://arxiv.org/abs/quant-ph/9709032v1 >.

Tegmark, M.: 1999, " The importance of quantum decoherence in brain processes", <https://arxiv.org/abs/quant-ph/9907009>.

Tegmark, M.: 2003, "Parallel Universes", <http://space.mit.edu/home/tegmark/PDF/multiverse_sciam.pdf>.

Tegmark, M.: 2007, "Many Lives in Many Worlds", *Nature*, 448, 23, July 2007, <arXiv.org/abs/0707.2593v1>.

Tegmark, M.: 2010, "Many Worlds in Context", <arxiv.org/abs/0905.2182v2>.

Tegmark, M.: 2014, *Our Mathematical Universe*, Vintage Books, New York.

Vaidman, L.: 2002, "Many-Worlds Interpretation of Quantum Mechanics", *The Stanford Encyclopedia of Philosophy*, Edward N. Zalta (ed.), <https://plato.stanford.edu/archives/sum2002/entries/qm-many-worlds/>.

von Baeyer, H.: 2013, "Quantum Weirdness? It's All in Your Mind", *Scientific American*, 308, 46-51, New York.

von Baeyer, H.: 2016, *Qbism: The Future of Quantum Physics*, Harvard University Press.

von Neumann, J.: 1932, *Mathematische Grundlagen der Quantenmechanik*, Springer, Berlin, English Translation by Beyer, R., *Mathematical Foundations of Quantum Mechanics*, Princeton University Press, 1955.

Wallace, D.: 2011, "Decoherence and Ontology, or: How I Learned To Stop Worrying And Love FAPP ", <http://arxiv.org/abs/1111.2189>.

Weyl, H.: 1934, *Mind and Nature*, University of Pennsylvania Press, Philadelphia.

Weyl, H.: 1949, *Philosophy of Mathematics and Natural Science*, Princeton University Press, Princeton.

West, J. 2009, "On the Gnostic Trinity", <https://ogdoas.wordpress.com/2012/09/17/on-the-gnostic-trinity/>.

Wheeler, J.: 1986, How Come the Quantum? New Techniques and Ideas in Quantum Measurement Theory, *Annals of the New York Academy of Sciences*, 480, 304-16.

Wheeler, J. & Ford, K.: 1998, *Geons, Black Holes, and Quantum Foam: A Life in Physics*, W.W. Norton & Co., New York.

Wigner, E.: 1961, "Remarks on the mind-body question", in *Symmetries and Reflections*, I. J. Good, ed. The Scientist Speculates, Basic Books, New York.

Wilczek, F.: 2006, *Fantastic Realities*, World Scientific Publishing, Singapore.

Zeh, D.: 1970, "On the interpretation of measurement in quantum theory", *Foundations of Physics*, March 1970, Volume 1, Issue 1, pp 69–76, Springer, Berlin.

Images

Images derived from:

Double Slit Water Waves, 2019, B. Crowell, <https://phys.libretexts.org/@api/deki/files/1381/double-slit-water-waves.png?revision=1&size=bestfit&width=226&height=169>, Licensed under CC-BY-SA.

Quantum Cartoon - Level 3, 2003, Tegmark, M., "Parallel Universes", <http://arxiv.org/abs/astro-ph/0302131v1>.

Schrodingers cat, 2008, Wikimedia User: 'Dhatfield', <http://en.wikipedia.org/wiki/File:Schrodingers_cat.svg>, Licensed under CC BY-SA 3.0.

Lorenz Attractor, 2013, D. Quinn, <https://upload.wikimedia.org/wikipedia/commons/1/13/A_Trajectory_Through_Phase_Space_in_a_Lorenz_Attractor.gif>, Licensed under CC BY-SA 3.0.

Biographies are depicted as lines through a cylinder, parallel in the sides, 1989, p. 132, M. Lockwood, *Mind, Brain & the Quantum*, Blackwell, Oxford.

Worldline, 2005, Wikimedia User: 'SreeBot', <http://en.wikipedia.org/wiki/File:Brane-wlwswv.png>, Licensed under CC BY-SA 3.0.

Index

Note: Page numbers in bold type refer to main entries and definitions.

Printed in Great Britain
by Amazon

61438648R00120